Hear our pray

Zerah A.

WAIT—DON'T PULL THAT PLUG!

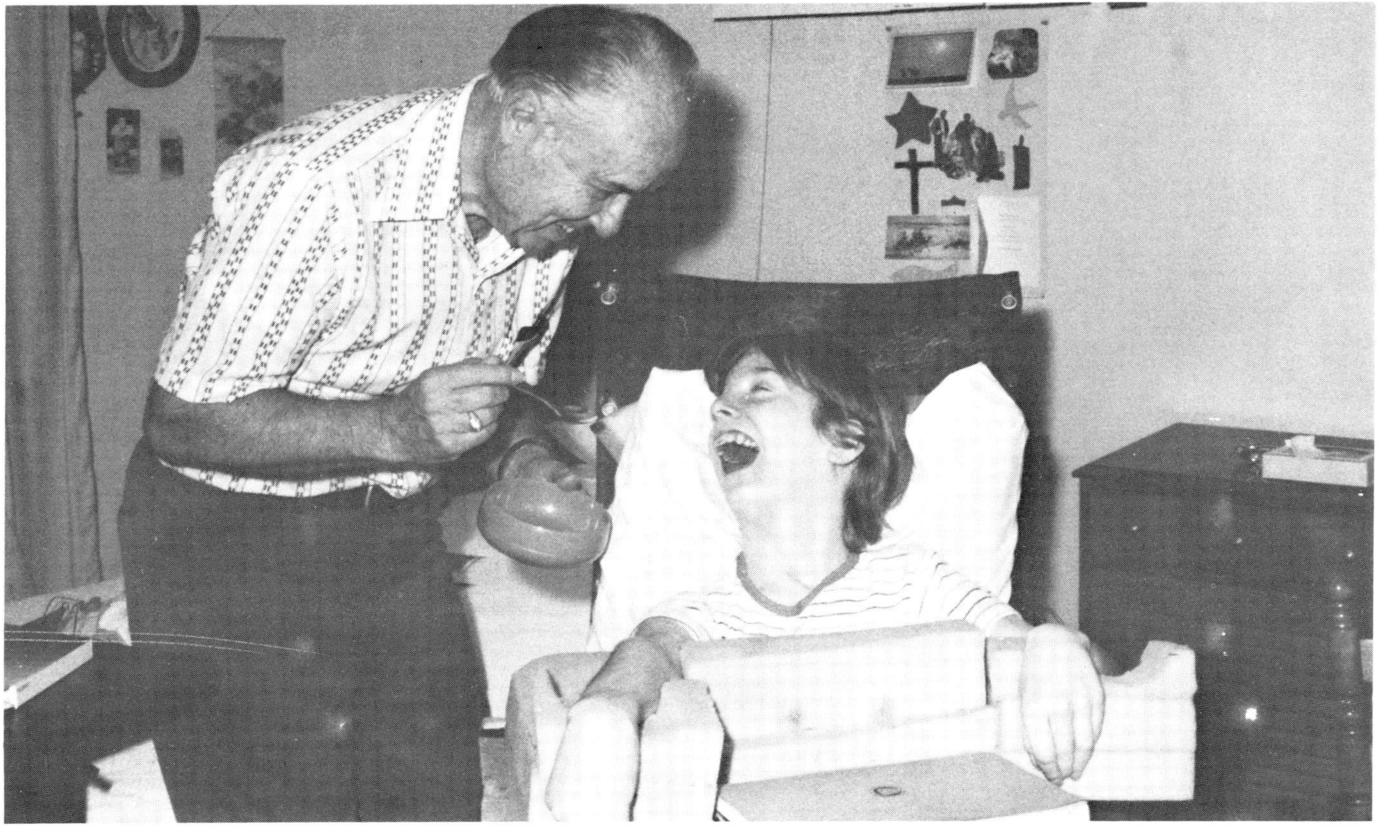

The author feeds Timmy his beloved ice cream

Wait—
Don't Pull That Plug!

The Story of Timmy

ZERAH A. CAMPBELL

EXPOSITION PRESS
HICKSVILLE, NEW YORK

FIRST EDITION

ISBN 0-682-49278-7

Printed in the United States of America

To my son,
Eugene,
and
to the memory
of my wife,
Madge

CONTENTS

PREFACE

This is a story about Timmy, who is fourteen years of age at this writing.

The author is hopeful that this book will be easily readable by adults, students, teenagers, and preadolescents.

As you journey with Timmy through his life struggles, please keep in mind that the story itself is factual as related by Timmy's friends and relatives. The author has deliberately put expressions in conversation as if they were Timmy's because of his inability to talk or write. For example, the beginning of chapter 1 expresses Timmy's feelings through the author's writing. The continual association with Timmy has helped the author to understand some of his thinking through facial, verbal, and eye expressions.

Students of psychology should recognize the happenings and results in their area of interest.

Those who are interested in medical science and related fields will find some examples in their realm.

Then we get to that wonderful word *love*, and to the results of sincere human affection. All of us should be involved in this category. The real meaning of *love* is given through our true love for one another, which means following the example of our religious leader of almost 2,000 years ago, who stressed the importance of loving our neighbors as ourselves.

After receiving the stimulus (from a brother-in-law) to write this real life story, I had no difficulty in arriving at the reasons for writing it. This type of story is needed in our society for various reasons: it is a far cry from sex-oriented stories, which are too plentiful; it may help us to understand the plights of others; and it might help us realize that we are not as bad off as we sometimes try to make ourselves believe. Also, this story may help all of us to use love in our lives more each day, as well as help us realize that others need our concern, attention, love, and prayer. I believe that intercessory prayer by each person who reads this story will help, not only Timmy, but also others who need prayers. Timmy needs help in many ways.

Let me point out that my conclusions, ideas, and phraseologies do not imply that all those who helped me or gave ideas to me agreed with my viewpoints as written in this book.

Actual names of individuals, except the author's, have been changed to preserve their privacy.

I want to express my debt and gratitude to those who helped me in many ways. They include the following: the Bible; Eugene Campbell, Esq. (my son); the administrators, nurses, nurses aides, and general staff of the Colonial Manor Nursing Home (York, Pennsylvania); an elementary school supervisor and teacher, both of whom wish to remain anonymous; Gold Photography (York, Pennsylvania); Timmy's parents and siblings; the Pennsylvania State Police office; Timmy's physicians; Randy Ruth; Thayer Sieg; Dr. Robert Terry (professor); Dr. Elton Trueblood (philosopher and writer); the Wilmac Corporation (York, Pennsylvania); and York Hospital.

All those who wish to may write to Timmy at the Colonial Manor Nursing Home, 970 Colonial Avenue, York, Pennsylvania, 17403.

WAIT—DON'T PULL THAT PLUG!

1

THAT AWFUL DAY

4:10 P.M., Sunday, September 28, 1975

It was six days after my twelfth birthday. The sun was shining brightly and I was outside enjoying it. I darted across Route 30 in southeastern Pennsylvania. Suddenly I heard the screeching of tires and the honking of horns, and I saw a big dark object—I wasn't sure of the color—obstructing my progress. Something had to give, so what chance did I have?

The driver did not have time to avoid me. The monster socked me with its right front fender, picked me up like a sack of wheat, bounced me off the hood and into the windshield like a rubber ball, and flung me up and over the roof. The driver ducked as I went by. Then with a thump I hit the rear bumper, which gently laid me as a lump of clothing and broken bones on the hard concrete floor of the highway.

I lay motionless. The world was dark—so dark—whereas just a few seconds before the sun had been shining. I had been waiting for my idol, Dandy, to come home (Dandy is a race driver). Perish the thought that I may never see him again.

"Is he dead?" "Call a doctor, quick." "Is he breathing?" "I couldn't help it. I'm so sorry."

A lady was crying and sobbing hysterically.

"Call an ambulance. Call the police!"

All of these voices sounded frantic in their appeals—but too late now. Just one second would have made a difference.

"This highway should be a four-lane highway instead of a three-lane throughway."

Where is my mother? Where is my brother Hank? I thought I was talking but no one was answering any of my questions.

One vehicle had tried to kill me and now another vehicle is hauling me away at a high rate of speed with the sirens screaming to try to save my life. I had always liked to hear sirens so now I hear them continually—but they're hurting my ears. Stop, please stop them!

I stop breathing and I ask WHY? Why are they trying to get me to breathe again?—I don't want to live because I hurt so much. I'm breathing again. Oh, please stop those searing noises of the siren. I've stopped breathing again. Oh no, too much pain, I can't stand it. Good-bye Hank, good-bye Mom, good-bye Dandy, good-bye Ginie, good-bye Artie, good-bye Dad, good-bye everyone.

I'm in a hospital—the emergency room. Oh no, I'm not breathing again. That makes three times that I have died. Please let me die. But they won't. I am unable to talk so they are doing just what they want to do.

I don't know how long I was in the emergency room but I now find myself in the intensive care unit of the hospital. There is a tube in my throat that will be my partner for the next several weeks.

I hear no one as I lay with my eyelids closed and my brain damaged. Somehow I'm still breathing, with the help of a respirator together with the tube in my throat. Please, someone, pull the plug to this respirator. I have so much pain. I can't stand it. I want to die. I have a little feeling. I felt pain when someone applied pressure to my legs while placing one in traction and the other one in a cast. I notice that my left leg is curved outward from my knee to the top of my toes, and that my right leg is worse because the ankle is at least four times as large as normal. Also, bones seem ready to protrude up through the skin—WHAT A SIGHT!

My face is sore from abrasions and cuts caused when I came in contact with the concrete highway. I feel a throb in my badly bruised right thigh. My eyeballs are jumping like fireflies in the night. Someone lifts my eyelids frequently and finds unequal and poorly reactive pupils, no corneal reflexes nor doll's eyes. I shake at times with contractions of the upper extremities—more on my right than on my left. I hear voices and remarks that lead me to believe that my brain is severely damaged, if not completely destroyed. This darn tube in my nose bothers me, but I can't complain because I can't say a single word.

I'm tired. I want to sleep, but someone keeps bothering me. Now there's a tube that goes into my bladder—I know what that is for. You see, that becomes number four in the number of tubes, which includes the tube in my arm that feeds me, to keep me alive. WHY?

Now it is quiet so I can relax and sleep for a while—I hope to eternity. Why, oh why, did it happen? Too late now. I hope that other children are more careful than I was when they cross the streets or highways. Please be careful, don't get in the same shape as I.

Now old times flash through my mind. How vividly I remember one morning when I woke up and saw the face of Dad instead of Mom.

"Where's Mom?" I asked with my eyes half-open.

"She's gone," said Dad with a quiet, sad voice. "I guess that she does not want to live with us anymore." Dad tried to hold back the tears that were forming in his eyes, and being a man he was doing pretty good.

"But, Dad, please say it isn't true. I'm only three. I'll miss her so much. Doesn't she love me anymore?" By now I was crying and the words stopped.

"We'll make it, kid, we'll make it somehow," Dad said as he kissed me and patted me on top of the head in his usual way. But this time he was very sad as he talked.

Dad stayed home from work for a couple of days in order to get our home reorganized and to see that all of us were getting a proper start in the mornings. My brothers and sisters were old enough to go to school at this time.

A neighbor lady came over often and said that she would help me. Sometimes she would take the washing, which Dad had put up before going to work in the morning, off the clothesline. Dad also did much of the cooking and caring for all of our family. Poor Dad.

Baby-sitters, many of them, tried to care for me while Dad was at work, but I hated them, all of them. No other female took the place of Mom. After throwing objects, insults, and tantrums, and kicking frequently for a few weeks, Dad had no other choice but to leave me home by myself all day long while he worked and my brothers and sisters were in school. I drank milk and ate hot dogs (is there such a thing as a *cold* hot dog? Ha Ha!). Well, I got tired of hot dogs. Can you imagine a kid getting tired of hot dogs?

We lived in the country with a loose gravel road in front of our house. So what did I do to keep out of mischief? I picked up small pebbles and threw them at the cars going by. Then I would run up the hill, across the road, and hide behind old cemetery headstones. Did I say "keep out of mischief"? I never hurt anyone by doing this. I got my stepbrother Artie in trouble more than once by egging him on to throw the stones as I picked them up and handed them to him. My excuse was that he could throw better than I could.

One day Artie and I climbed up a tree by the roadside in front of our house and then poured water on a car that was going by. The driver stopped, got out of the car, and yelled at us, but we just crawled up higher in the tree. I doubt if the driver of that car ever knew what kind of water we dumped—well or urine.

My daydreaming is over for now because here comes a lady in white again—it's amazing what one can see *through* the eyelids. The nurse is very nice and somewhat pretty.

"H'mm, high fever," she mutters.

"Why not, with all I've gone through," I try to say.

"No reaction yet," she continues, as she raises my eyelids.

"Now this is to remain for a while against the outer left leg to try to avoid so much external rotation," says a young man who had carried a sandbag into my room and placed it on my bed.

I'm sleepy now and my head hurts, in fact I hurt all over. Guess I'll get a wink or two before someone else disturbs me.

Hope that I will sleep for a long time.

2

A BIG DAY

Let's permit Timmy to sleep for a while as you and I meditate. Is there a pattern for our lives to follow?

Have you ever said to yourself or to others, "What is to be will be," and then lived according to that statement? Then, when something happens that adversely affects your way of living, do you ask, "Why me? Why did it happen to ME?"

After a seemingly endless space of time we decide that we need an uplift from someone or somewhere. Where should we turn? In what direction must we go? Who will help us? In these instances, I pick up the book that has been a best seller for years and that has withstood criticism, ridicule, questioning, and misunderstanding as well as a great amount of understanding—the Bible. I turn to Proverbs and finally come across the thirteenth verse of chapter 15 in the New American Standard Bible. I read once, and I re-read, again and again—"A joyful heart makes a cheerful face, but when the heart is sad, the spirit is broken." Think about that message, then turn it around and see what you get and what happens if you believe.

After a series of four trips to the operating room of a large, city-sized hospital in February and March of 1976, the following came as a severe shock one morning: "You are being released from this hospital today. You are to go home." A doctor with cold, black, penetrating eyes stared at me for a while.

"But, Doc, I can't walk yet. I can't go home in this condition. My wife is not living and I just can't get along." I begged desperately.

"Check with him later in the day, but he is to be released today," the doctor said, meeting a nurse in the doorway. The nurse came over to my bed and, as she saw that I was quite disturbed, tried to console me.

"Please talk to him again." I pleaded with the nurse. "I can only get around with a walker, and even then the pain is almost unbearable." I talked to deaf ears.

My fine son arranged for me to enter a nursing home that had a highly recommended physical therapy department and an excellent group of workers who had the welfare of the patient at heart. But let me add that I did not go *home* from the hospital nor did I leave the hospital that day to go to the *nursing home*, but I did check out the following day.

A beautiful young lady with blond hair—my weakness was for blond females, even though I had married a brunette—was my guide and helper in the therapy department at the nursing home. But alas, I discovered that she was happily married, and too young for me anyway. Would psychologists call that rationalization?

After a period of several emotional days in the nursing home, I was progressing satisfactorily with a walker. But I spent most of the day in a four-wheeled, hand-propelled wheelchair.

It was about noon one day when a member of the staff came to my room and asked me if I would visit a few patients inasmuch as I had established a rehabilitation program in another nursing home. After she told me the background of a few patients in particular she asked, "Will you visit with them a few times and then let me know what you think?"

"Not yet," I replied. "I would break down as I have been very sick and am still nervous and depressed. Numerous prescriptions had me "nuts" for a few weeks in the hospital—in fact, out of my mind—I am just now getting over some of those wild ideas and unbelievable trips. However, the cogs in my head still go around like a Ferris wheel in high gear."

"But will you go to see them at least three times in the near

(Oh, isn't it easy to complain about our problems when all we have to do is look just a stone's throw away and easily find those who are less fortunate or worse off than we.) Finally I went to sleep.

After breakfast and treatment in the physical therapy department, I came back to my room—in my wheelchair—and picked up the Bible, turning to the book of Matthew. I was trying to find a passage that I could use for the support I needed to fulfill my promise to see the two young people. I needed courage as well as relaxation to enter the room of these two severely injured victims of circumstance.

Here was the answer: "For I was hungry, and you gave Me something to eat; I was thirsty and you gave Me drink; I was a stranger, and you invited Me in; naked, and you clothed Me; I was sick, and you visited Me; I was in prison, and you came to Me." (Matthew 25:35-36, New American Standard Bible.) And when the disciples questioned Jesus as to when they had done these things to Him, Jesus replied, "Truly I say to you, to the extent that you did it to one of these brothers of Mine, *even* the least of *them*, you did it to Me." (Matthew 25:40, New American Standard Bible.)

That was the answer to my delayed decision. I called the person who had asked me to do the visiting, and I told her that I was ready to visit the young men. "Tomorrow is the day," I said. "In the afternoon."

"All right, that is just fine. I will come to your room right after lunch and push you and the wheelchair to the proper room."

The morning of The Big Day. Almost too quickly after I enjoyed a fine lunch, the afternoon arrived. I needed composure. I prayed, "Help me, Lord." As I look back, the trip to the appointed room was simple and easy; but what I saw there will always leave a deep impression and, yes, depression in my wrinkled brain.

"Here we are, Mr. Campbell," said a sweet voice that seemed to be miles away.

Mark, the patient nearest the door, was the twenty-six-year-old. His dark brown eyes were fixed and staring, his arms were in a fixed but straight position on top of the covers, his covered legs were apparently inactive (I did not notice any movement whatsoever). I spoke to Mark, but received no response other than the stare of his bulging pupils. I held his right hand and talked to him—no response. Then I held his left hand, and received an ever-so-little squeeze. I was to get just slightly more of a reaction in the future months that I saw him. I was reminded that he had suffered severe brain damage caused by going headfirst through the windshield of his car, landing headfirst in a pasture of rock and dirt. I can imagine that his head was pile-driven—terrible!

I turned my wheelchair and went to the other patient—Timmy.

Little did I dream that April 14, 1976, would be a day to remember forever in my life. I turned to face the rear of the lowered back of another wheelchair. *What am I to see? What do I expect? What will I say? What will I do?* I wanted to leave the room but I couldn't. Something would not let me reverse the chair and start for the door. *How long will I stay?* What seemed like eternity, as I sat motionless in my chair, was probably just a single tick of a clock. A nurse was preparing something near the window by a table while the beautiful brunette staff member was by my side. I looked up at her and was greeted with an assuring smile and a wink of her left eye. (Can you wink with your left eye?)

"This is Timmy," she said softly as she pushed my chair to the right side in front of Timmy's chair.

"Oh, no!" my mind shouted inaudibly. What I saw was a torture-laden lad—nothing there, apparently, except skin and bones. Oh, yes, I saw some beautiful hair. Did I say beautiful? Yes, that is what I just saw, and immediately like a flash of lightning the room was light and beautiful, and things were changing. There is something beautiful in the worst of us! Here was a nice-looking lad of about twelve with clear, fair skin. His sandy-hued, slightly curly hair was beautiful—somewhat long but not hippie-long. He was almost in a reclining position, about two-thirds flat on his back, sitting up so slightly.

I saw his beautiful but pain-racked face. His head was twisted to the extreme left in a fixed position. Before looking at his eyes I noticed saliva slowly running from the left corner of his mouth to his chest like a silk thread. Time out. I needed to take a couple of deep breaths.

My eyes wandered. I saw two immovable hands in a groping, twisted position against the boy's chest. His hands, with the fingers almost touching the wrists in a rigid, fixed position, lay almost touching each other. His arms lay crosswise, almost touching his chest. There was no movement in his arms, nor in stiffened, frozen-looking fingers.

I maneuvered to the other side of his chair and stopped in front of this lad. I saw beauty in his face, but the details that I also saw were disheartening and unbelievable—they might never be erased from my mind.

As you recall, his head was twisted to the left side, and was fixed there; saliva, like a hot thread you might notice when cooking candy, ran frequently but slowly from the left corner of his open mouth—which he could not close. One to two inches separated his lower lip from his upper lip—this was one of many conditions long to be endured. His breathing was noticeable because it was through his mouth, and slightly audible, like a slight cold.

There was no sign of recognition as I looked into his eyes—two eyes moving continually in uncoordinated circles, first clockwise and then counterclockwise, but at a pace leading one to believe that one corner of each eyeball was chasing the other corner—just wild moving and wild staring. Again I gazed ever so quickly at his deformed hands, fingers, wrists, and arms. It was unbelievable that all of this could happen to one person, but there he was—just like that.

I talked to Timmy but received no answer—not even a quieting of the eyes or a movement of any bones.

"Would you care to see Timmy's legs?" a nurse asked.

"Yes," I replied hesitantly, fearing what I might see as there had not been any noticeable movement for the few minutes that I had been in the room.

The covers were pulled slowly back from the feet. I almost gasped (but did not dare in Timmy's presence), as I saw two curved legs with the right ankle out of shape and deformed—it appeared that the right ankle was at least three times its normal size. I can imagine that my eyes were moving in fast circles to coincide with my brain. Timmy would close his eyelids frequently and then reopen them quickly for me to see those eyes racing like bats flitting here and there in the night. Eyeballs and eyelids were the only moving parts of that entire body.

I stayed about two hours (or was it only ten minutes), talking with Timmy but receiving no response as I spoke or moved while in my wheelchair. I had related to Timmy my name and told him why I was in the wheelchair. I repeated his name and my name many times during this and future sessions. Someone told me that his prognosis was that his present condition would be *as is, this is his limit*—he would probably be a complete vegetable as long as he lived.

I was assisted quietly back to my room—the nicely carpeted hallway in the nursing home deferred the ease of wheeling one's self in a wheelchair, but it was good exercise for the hands and arms to try nevertheless. The hundred-foot trip to my room was made without a word being spoken by the staff member or myself.

"Thanks for helping me," I said. "I'll see you tomorrow."

"Okay. Shall it be the same time as today?"

"That will be fine, and thanks again," I murmured.

I had learned a certain landmark to identify my room. A flaming red housing was to the upper left corner of the outside of the door to my room, or home for the next few weeks. This fixture was the fire alarm. Do you want to know what happened one night?

One quiet evening about eleven o'clock, when only a few loud snores were penetrating the stillness and darkness of a dimly lighted hallway, a series of alarms and clangs let loose. You can imagine the loudness in my room, since the sound came from the red housing just outside my door. In a few seconds, I heard the sirens of fire engines getting nearer and nearer so I immediately began to figure out a way of escaping. Beads of perspiration were on my forehead and my body was beginning to feel very moist. I glanced to the left of my bed, where three windows gave me light in the daytime. I quickly decided to use my crutches, which were in the corner near my bed, to smash one of the windows. I would then drop the few feet to the ground—I had it figured out in a matter of seconds. But the fire trucks soon left and my excitement and nervousness disappeared when an aide quietly and slowly reopened my door.

Okay, I got off my prior trend of thought, but I hope that you are back with me as I lie in bed rehashing the events of the past day. I'm thinking of those two young men down the hall who are in an almost helpless and hopeless condition. WHY? Why did those accidents have to happen? After periods of tossing in bed I finally went to sleep and spent a very restless night. I still had difficulty turning from side to side in my bed, but used the bed rails satisfactorily. Even so, it was an effort to shift my weight when in a reclining position. When I did turn I thought of Mark and Timmy, who were not able to turn.

"Ready for breakfast?" asked a sweet voice.

"Sure am," I replied, not knowing what was on the plate under the metal cover. I was still half-asleep.

"I hope that you will enjoy everything this morning, and be sure to eat all of it." The young lady in white left me after she raised the head of my bed.

"Thanks very much," I replied, with my thoughts still wandering down the hall. I wondered what Mark and Timmy were eating and who was feeding them.

I went to the physical therapy rooms at nine o'clock and got back to my room about eleven. Then I had a good lunch.

"Are you ready, Mr. Campbell?" The staff member was ready to assist me in the *long* one hundred feet to see the boys.

"Okay, let's go. I'm as ready as I'll ever be."

"Don't you want to go today?" she asked.

"Oh, sure I do," I quickly replied. I felt that I *must* go. Something urged me—really pulled at me.

We traveled rapidly down the hall, and this day turned

out to be the same as the first day except that I seemed to be accustomed to the environment and conditions already. I spoke to each of the young men and talked for a few minutes in an attempt to get some reaction. I watched intently and with wide-open eyelids so that I would not miss any reaction. My eyes became tired after a few minutes of this because I hesitated to close my eyelids even for a second for fear of missing any reaction. I called each one by his correct name and also mentioned mine, as it was necessary for recall—if any was there.

On the sixth day after my first visit I still was not progressing with Mark—only a slight squeeze of his left hand when I asked him to do so when I spoke. But, with Timmy, I was to be shocked.

"Timmy, if you hear me, please close your eyes." My head dropped quickly and moisture glistened in my eyes as Timmy immediately closed his eyelids and then reopened them, revealing those ever-wild, chasing eyes. Didn't his eyes ever get tired? He responded twice that same day in response to my requests. I did not ask him to respond a third time because I did not want him to get tired and restless, or ultimately uninterested.

Each day as I entered their room I said, "Hi Mark, Hi Timmy." Then I would say my name at least two times. I tried to show a personal interest in each one, but what do you talk about when you do not get any replies and do not know their interests?

Daily, Timmy responded to my question, "Timmy, if you hear me, will you please close your eyes?" Then, on April 25, I was pleasantly surprised again when I asked the following question: "Timmy, will you please smile if you hear me?" The already-open mouth spread more in size and each corner widened as if in a smile. Oh, wonderful! I tried it once more that day and received the correct response. Was I right in my belief that there was a part of his brain that was still working?

Finally, and this day was to be a very difficult one for me, it was necessary for me to tell both Mark and Timmy that I was going home the next day.

So, on April 29, 1976, I told the more unfortunate lads that

I was getting along so well with my walking that I was going home to fend for myself as best I could with the help of a cane.

"Good-bye, Mark." He squeezed my hand and did not want to let go. I never saw Mark again.

"Good-bye, Timmy." I choked. "Will you smile for me?" He responded immediately and correctly.

After I told them that I would be back to see each one when I was able to drive my car and get around, I left the room with my cane in hand. I was very low in spirit and I am sure that a few drops of clear liquid ran down and over my cheeks.

After a summer of satisfactory recuperation, I finally discarded the cane and walked slowly without any artificial help.

Fall came, and one day I felt an impulse—an impulse that found me driving my car toward that nursing home—one of the best I have ever visited or entered. I have told my son that this home above all homes is to be used for me, if I ever have to return for necessary care.

To avoid bothering you with dates as to when I visited the home and Timmy, just go along with me as I tell you that I attempted to make a visit once a week for many months to come.

3

IN THE HOSPITAL

Shall we allow Timmy to take over for a while as he talks inaudibly to himself in the nursing home?

Here I am, unable to talk or move at all. I suffer, but the nurses do not know it because I have no way to tell them. Sometimes the pain is terrible but no one knows but me.

Where is that man who used to come in and talk with me? Oh yes, he said that he was going home. Has he forgotten me? Won't he ever come back to talk with me? Doesn't anyone care to see me? I know that I must be a terrible-looking sight but I can't help it now. I guess the nurses and aides must think that I don't comprehend when they are talking. I still don't know why I'm here in the nursing home. I thought that I was in the hospital. What really happened? Please tell me, someone. I guess that I have forgotten.

My brain has cobwebs in it—many cobwebs—but I do hear and understand a little of the whispering and talking by the aides and nurses.

My mother just walked in. How do I know? Well, my right eye sees only a dim outline of people but I do recognize her voice. Mom and a nurse are talking about my condition and the accident. Accident? What accident? Oh yes, it was an accident. I have heard and remember some of the things that I am hearing now but people seem to like to repeat incidents that are out of the ordinary.

Mom is talking. "Timmy wanted to go with a friend and me on a Sunday, September 28, 1975, but I told him that he was to stay home with his brother and sister this time. Timmy said, 'Okay, Mom,'—those were the last words he spoke to me.

"Timmy was waiting for his race driver idol, Dandy, to come home in the afternoon. He was attempting to cross the heavily traveled road, and a car hit him. He liked to help the race driver empty the truck and then clean the race car when Dandy got home from racing." Mom was crying.

"Did you see him right away in the emergency room at the hospital?" asked the nurse.

"No, we did not get home until some time later, at which time we were notified of the accident. We went to the hospital right away."

"Was he unconscious at the time?" the other voice asked.

"Oh, yes," Mom continued. "There was a tube in his throat. I was told that he had stopped breathing three times before I got to the hospital."

I hope that no one took a picture of me in that emergency room. Can you picture a lad of twelve with the following conditions all at one time?

UNRESPONSIVE ON RESPIRATOR—what does that mean?

TRACHEOTOMY INCISION—I know what *incision* means, but not the other word. Then there were many tubes sticking out of my body.

Mom was talking again. She said that she remembered that I was unresponsive to pressure or pain. Oh, if she only knew that I really suffered pain all over. I guess that I was just plain numb in many places.

"Were there any deep cuts or scratches?" the nurse asked.

You understand, don't you, why the nurse was asking many questions? I was in the nursing home many months after the accident happened, and I had time to heal in certain spots from minor ailments.

"No, no really deep cuts, just a few abrasions from the rough pavement." Mom added, "I'm still concerned about his eyes, they are never still. I was told at the hospital that both eyes were unresponsive for quite some time—and finally only the right eye began to show some movement or reaction to stimuli."

"What else did the doctors tell you about Timmy's condition?"

"Well," Mom was sobbing again, "he suffered severe trauma."

What in the heck is *trauma* I wondered.

"Oh, I recall that there were a few bruises over his scalp and the sides of his face plus bruises on the right medial thigh."

"Did they try to do something with his hands and legs?" asked the nurse. "How bad were they at the beginning?"

"Well," Mom was almost whispering, "his left leg was grossly deformed, with internal rotation and shortening; the right leg was also grossly deformed with lateral rotation, and the right ankle was extremely out of shape and enlarged considerably. One day I was told that the prognosis was very grave."

What, I wondered is *prognosis*? Does it have something to do with my nose? I'll find out some day.

The nurse then told Mom that she would read some of my history on the nursing home records.

After a few minutes, conversation led me to believe that I had been in the intensive care unit at the hospital for quite some time. I remember that I was bothered very much by someone taking my temperature and checking the many tubes in my body.

Mom continued speaking lightly and quietly. "His Dad and I visited Timmy frequently, but on every visit we were led to believe that the odds were against him, that he would never recover, and that his present condition was at a low ebb. We were braced for the worst at all times."

I guess that everyone thought I was going to die for sure.

"When did you begin to receive encouragement from his very slightly improved condition?" Mom was asked.

"Well, after many days Timmy began to respond to painful stimuli."

Well, who wouldn't jump or twitch when a needle was jabbed into his skin and muscles, or when he was subjected to an operation to put in a tube without first being put to sleep?

While Mom and the nurse continued to talk I began to feel sleepy—or was I daydreaming?

I'm back in the hospital several weeks ago and my mind is confused but I do remember some things. My eyes are a blank and I am barely able to move my right arm. But nothing else will move, even though I try very hard.

I am beginning to respond to touch, and I am making some sucking motions with my wide-open mouth. Am I hungry? I'm always hungry! Why can't I close my mouth and put my lips together? I try but with no success.

"He's got a high fever!" a nurse almost shouts. "Over 102." Is that bad? But I later hear conversations that my fever went up and down for a few weeks—it had some people puzzled, I guess.

Now they are sticking another tube into me, this time in a vein in my right side to measure some fluids, I guess.

"His fever is higher today," exclaims a nurse as she removes a thermometer from my mouth. "I had better notify the doctor at once." In a few minutes she brings in some ice bags to help adjust my fluctuating fever.

One day an extra helper came into my room and, seeing a thermometer in my *mouth*, exclaimed "Who did that, why this thermometer is a *rectal* one." Ha! Ha! Just one of my jokes.

"Ten days after entering the intensive care unit at the hospital," my Mom was saying again at the nursing home, "his right pupil reacted sluggishly to light, but the left pupil was dilated and nonreactive. Someone applied a sandbag to his outer leg because of the external rotation."

"Didn't they work on his legs and arms at the hospital?" asked the nurse. "Wasn't any kind of therapy used?"

"Yes," Mom replied quickly, "about eighteen days after his admission to the hospital a skeletal traction was placed on his left leg and a short leg cast on his right leg. At the same time, his elbow joints became very rigid. Yes, some therapy was given for a short time."

This is me again, Timmy that is. Oh, I wish that Mr. Campbell would come in to be with me for a while. I'm getting so tired of hearing about what happened to me. *Let* me alone. Yes, and *leave* me alone, too. I wish that they would go out of my room so I would not hear them talking about me. No one was concerned about me when I was well. Oh, I guess they really were, but at that time I felt that I was alone in this world. I guess that people did talk about me when I was unruly or misbehaved. My Dad corrected me harshly at times, but maybe I had it coming.

I did some crazy things, but didn't other kids? I remember one time that my brother and I were "sweet-hungry." It so happened that a few feet right in front of us was a bread and cake delivery truck. No one was around, so we ran to the open rear door of the truck and, before you could snap your fingers a couple of times, we had our hands full of little cakes and packages of cookies—and we were on our way in a hurry, believe me. We were punished for this in a manner befitting kids of nine.

The nurse is talking again. "When did the attendants at the hospital notice any reaction whatsoever to verbal stimuli?"

"About a month after the accident," said Mom. "He began to be more alert and he held onto a nurse's hand. The nurse mentioned that Timmy seemed to understand but without any response—physical response."

About forty-four days later, while I was still at the hospital, my left eye was moving laterally some, and physical therapy was then started. Then, four days later, a nurse thought that she heard a moan—the first noise from me—when a new catheter was inserted.

Another twelve days passed before a doctor suggested that he did not want to put splints on my lower extremities. Also on this day someone made a suggestion that a hospital staff member should write to a social service consultant for possible nursing home placement in the near future. I was placed in a wheelchair for about fifteen minutes daily for the next several days. Every day found me in a wheelchair, coughing and perspiring, for short periods of time. I also vomited frequently, especially while sitting up in a wheelchair.

Finally, the tube in my neck was removed—it had been a long time since September 28. Then, three days later, I tried to scream with happiness when the tube feeding was stopped. I wondered when they would start feeding me hamburgers, french fried potatoes, and milk shakes? Little did I know then that many moons would rise and set before I would enjoy those items, if ever. I coughed with every bite of baby food—it was very difficult to swallow.

Before the accident, I used to watch birds as they dipped their beaks to grab a swallow of water, just a drop I guess, but I finally knew how much a drop of water was when it went down my throat. However, I did have at least one advantage over a bird. Notice a bird when it feeds or drinks? It takes just one dip of the beak to swallow, and then it raises its head to be aware of probable danger. We humans have that part easier, don't we?

One hundred and eleven days after admisssion to the hospital

I had been under "routine care" for some time. This was the day that someone put a note on my thick and voluminous—where did that big word come from?—book of charts, "If no fever in forty-eight hours, discharge to a nursing home." So four days later, and 115 days after that TERRIBLE DAY, I was transferred to a nursing home in a comatose condition. As with all comatose patients, I was without response to my external environment.

I am now in a fine nursing home after leaving the hospital a short time ago. How long will I be here? Am I to be a vegetable as long as I live? Some think that I will, I'm sure. What do people mean when they use the word *vegetable* when referring to people? I had heard *that* word used by Mom and Dad and various nurses. A vegetable is something to eat but they do grow to a certain limit—is that for me? What is my limit? Will I grow anymore? Will I get taller? Will I ever shave like Dad does? Will I ever be able to play baseball like some of my baseball heroes? Will my mind grow to maturity? Am I getting a negative answer? Perish the thought.

4

PLAYFUL TIMES

Now that medical science has done so much for me, has it reached its limits? I know that I would not be alive today if many fine medical people had not helped me and used their minds and the fine instruments that someone provided.

What is left? Struggle in this condition? Sleep away—DIE? I remember Dad talking about Jesus healing and performing miracles. Dad used to have Bible study in our home at least once a week. He also mentioned that many evangelists were performing miracles through the power of Jesus. Am I a probable candidate for a miracle? But I can't talk to anyone—not even to Jesus. No sound comes out of my throat. When will I talk? Ever? HELP ME SOMEONE, PLEASE!

I suffer and have pain, but no one knows because I am unable to tell anyone. What is there for me in this condition? I want love! I want affection! I NEED affection! Please! Someone! My mind is begging. Yes, my heart is begging. Many people beg with their hands or their voices, but poor me, only my mind can beg. Or do I have a mind—is it a vegetable? Now I am beginning to realize what the nurses meant when they talked about my being a vegetable. Is my brain dead? No! I know what is going on, only I can't talk or move any part of my body. Oh boy, what a mess I'm in, just because I tried to outrun a car. Let this be a lesson to those who attempt to rush too much too soon to beat a vehicle, whether they are on foot, riding a two-wheeler, riding a three-wheeler, using a skateboard or driving a car.

I'm tired so I think that I will sleep for a while. Some wild dreams, such as a fly trying to work its way out of a spider's web, run in and out of my mind. I always laughed when I saw the spider finally grab the fly, and I laughed more when I squashed the spider.

Artie is my stepbrother. He is about my age but a little bit stronger. One day he and I ran out of the house at the rear of our yard (our outhouse, or outside toilet). We ran alongside a creek to a bridge not far from our house. As we ran in and out of the stream, getting our shoes wet without concern, we saw a moving object up ahead.

"What's that, Artie?" I asked excitedly.

"Don't know," he replied. "But let's find out, eh?"

"Let's grab a couple of sticks to fight with in case it makes a dash for us. Okay?" I really was excited by this time.

We walked slowly toward the object almost like a cat approaching a bird.

"Oh, it's a groundhog!" yelled Artie.

"Golly, it's big. It will bite us." I jumped behind Artie.

"Don't do that, Timmy, he's not hurting you," snapped Artie as I started to beat the poor defenseless animal. "Anyway, we can run faster than he can if he should start to chase us. STOP!"

"This is fun," I said laughingly, as I continued to hit at the groundhog.

"If you don't stop doing that I'm going to sock you and take that stick away from you," shouted Artie angrily.

What did I do? In the first place, I ignored Artie's threats. The next thing I knew I was punching out the eyes of the poor animal, who was there to find food and water with no intent to harm anyone. I laughed crazily while using the stick, but I cried later when I realized what I had done. I also cried even later, when Dad punished me.

Was I mean? No, just plain ornery, I guess.

I remember when I had the measles and mumps at an early age. Dad had quite a job just trying to keep me in bed for a few hours at a time, because I wanted to be up and around with the rest of the kids.

I guess that I had head congestion most of the time. It seems to bother me very much now, as I breathe through my throat and mouth because my nose seems to be clogged up. Anyway, my mouth is open all of the time because I am unable to close my lips—I don't know why I can't. I think that I would feel a little better if I could blow my nose but that doesn't seem possible either. I'm in a mess, ain't I? I can't even get my tongue to move to my teeth—it just lays flat on the bottom of my mouth.

Dad had an old-time remedy for the breaking out of the skin on my face—not pimples. Do you know what he did? Well, he would make me eat many oranges or grapefruit. This treatment seemed to do the trick.

Here I am, flat on my back in my room at the nursing home, where I receive wonderful treatment. No one is around to bother me now so I think that I will just relax as much as possible and think about more playful times I had when I was able to run around. Will I ever run again? Will I?

I liked to ice skate and roller skate. Will I ever be able to skate again? Sometimes I would ice skate for a while at the rink and then all of a sudden, without any premonition (where did that word come from?), I would start digging the ice with my skates. Then I would kick other kids as they skated by. Mean, wasn't I? Many times the manager, or the "mean guy" as I called him, would make me leave the rink. He "kicked" me off, huh?

My brother and I would go hunting with Dad, especially deer hunting. Dad tried to impress upon us that we should be as quiet as possible in order not to startle the deer—if there were any. Well, you know me, I would lag behind and intentionally step on branches and leaves in order to make noises. Was that the reason? Or did I want attention? Well, I got it from Dad, I'll tell you that. But honestly, I did want someone to know that I was along.

Grandma would talk with me many times when I visited her, but after a couple of days she seemed to get tired of my demand for her undivided attention most of the time. Then she would become a little irritable with me, although I know that she loved me—she told me so more than once.

Oh, oh, my daydreaming period is over for now because I just heard someone come into my room.

"Time to eat, Timmy," said a sweet voice. The voice was a welcome sound but the food was not as welcome because it was fed to me with a large syringe—it looked like a large hypodermic needle.

"Shoot it down my throat," I murmured to myself.

As the nurse fed me, some of the liquid food would run out of the corner of my mouth—you see I still was unable to move my head and it stayed in one position—to the left—all of the time.

"That's all, Timmy." It was the voice of the human feeder. "You did real well," she continued as she used a rough napkin to clean my lips and chin.

"Oh yeah," I thought. "I'm still hungry, especially for hamburgers and french fries and milk shakes. When will I get some of that junk?" No one but me knew that I was talking.

Guess I will do some more daydreaming. Do you want to hear about more of my playful times? Okay, here we go.

"Quack, quack, quack, quack," sounded some ducks as they chased me one day at the park because I had picked up some of their food and started to run away from them with it. Now I know just how they felt when someone takes away the food that I would like to have. It seems that I am hungry all of the time. I didn't eat any of the food I took from the ducks. I finally quit teasing them and threw the food at them. They quacked again when some of the food hit them.

"What are you doing that for?" yelled Grandma. "Stop that this instant!"

"I'm not hurting him," I quickly retorted loudly. Well, maybe I was hurting the family dog, Pal, a little as I grabbed tufts of hair and yanked them from him.

"Don't you ever let me catch you doing that again, young man." Grandma spoke in a stern way but with a pleasant voice.

Why are people always picking on me? They don't like me, I guess that's why. The dog receives more attention than I. The dog is shown more love and affection than is shown to me. The dog is kissed more often, too. Why?

Now I'm laughing, not aloud but enough so that I can feel my insides jumping even though my outer extremities are quiet—very quiet—I haven't moved them for several months. But what am I laughing about? Well, I remember that one day Mom took my older brother and me to a shopping area—mall I guess they call it—and we were to spend all day there, just roaming around and eating lunch.

"Now stay out of trouble, and be good," were Mom's parting words, as she gave us some money to spend and then drove away, leaving us in the parking lot. I always felt "big" when I had my own spending money.

"Okay," we both shouted as we waved good-bye. Oh yeah, all day by ourselves being good—what a laugh. That was really asking too much. I had too much energy to sit all day and do nothing. Some said that I was a mean child, but I said that it was just energy that I had to get rid of in some way. I always wanted to do something, be active—I was "hyper——." Maybe I should have been a little "hypo——" (psychologists, please fill in the blanks).

Well, anyhow, let's get back to that day when Mom left us at the mall to spend the day. We went into a large department store and roamed at will. My brother and I looked at some bottles of hair "stuff" and after-shave good-smelling liquid and underarm spray. I had never used any of that "junk," but it was fun for my brother and I to unscrew the caps of many cans and bottles and accidentally (?) upset the containers. Boy, was that a sweet-smelling place, with all of those perfumes and lotions dripping out of the cans and bottles onto the floor. FUN? You bet it was.

We thought that we had better move along to another store where we got really fiendish. We grabbed some tubes of "Vampire Blood" and squirted some on a mannequin and some on the clothes of some of the people in the store.

"Here comes the manager," my brother whispered as he took off.

"What are you kids doing here?" growled the manager.

"Nothing," I replied innocently. I just stood there, but my brother was somewhere else, out of sight by now.

"Now get out of here!" The manager was mad. "And I mean NOW!", he continued. He came close to me, as if to shove me or kick me out of the store.

I took off and started to run as the manager yelled, "And don't come back!"

He didn't touch me, but I left that store scuffing the toes of my shoes as I ran.

I guess my daydreaming is over for now because I just heard someone come into my room.

"Here are some pills, Timmy." The sweet, mild voice was somewhat different from the one I had just heard in the store in my daydream.

My eyes are not focusing yet, and all I can see is a darker-than-light image. I have begun to recognize voices though and I know when my food is to be served. Of course, I'm always hungry. When anyone says the word *eat*, I'm ready to go at it. I had trouble swallowing the pills that were broken up into small pieces. Then I realized that I wanted to relax and go to sleep for the night.

"Good morning, Timmy," said a female voice. It was familiar. Then I heard a noise and I knew that she was pulling the cord near the curtains so that the sun could smile upon my window-pane. There was more light in the room but I still could not see any objects distinctly. Someday I *will* see them—I know I will.

Today is almost gone and still no visit from that man who used to come and talk with me. I wonder how he is. Is he walking all right? Is he driving his car yet? He said that he would be back to see me. Why doesn't he come? I wish that I could talk so I could ask someone to call him and see if everything is all right with him.

Who's coming? Who just walked into my room? Those were strange footsteps. Those voices belong to Dad and my brother.

I smiled in the general direction of their voices, but I could not tell just what they looked like because they appeared just as images.

"Timmy," my brother was speaking, "remember the time that you and I were in a gameroom uptown and we were kicked out because you were caught punching holes in the ceiling with the billiard cue?"

"That was fun," I replied with no sound. "Yes, I remember that." But will I ever be able to go into that gameroom again? Will I ever play pool again? Will I ever be able to walk around a pool table? Will I ever use my hands again? They are immovable now, I can't even move any of my fingers.

"Oh, yes, I remember another time when you and I were just a little mean, Timmy," continued my brother. "That was the time when we were visiting Grandma, and we threw darts into the tires on the cars that were parked on the street near Grandma's house. It was fun listening to the air leaving the tires in a hissful sound."

Yes, I remembered, but all I could do was smile. Will I ever visit Grandma again?

After Dad and my brother left for the evening I soon relaxed and went into dreamland again. Dreamland would have been the only fun I had now except that the nurses and aides were so friendly and nice. They showed concern and affection at all times. I needed and wanted this love and affection and attention. I just couldn't lay there twenty-four hours, day and night, and not have anyone care if I was alive. If left alone, I might die. I once read about some animals that died when they were left alone for a long period of time with no one caring for or about them. They had been forsaken by their parents so I guess they had no reason to live.

But I'm not going to give up—NO SIR!

5

I NEED SOMETHING–WHAT?

Another day is here. I have been fed my breakfast—baby food and liquid. I will start taking physical therapy tomorrow—with what? But today, and especially now, I will just lay here and think. Of course I can think. I'm not a vegetable, at least not a complete vegetable. I know that I am not able to move any of my extremities but those wheels up in my head are moving and I hope that they don't ever stop.

But I need something. I not only *need* that something, but I *want* it. I want someone to love me and talk with me and know that I am here, physically helpless. Please, someone, pay at least some attention to me daily. I so want affection daily—even every minute. Hold my hands! Please, someone!

I want attention and I am going to get it. But how? Now as I think back about the mischievous things that I did, I ask myself why I did those things so often. I really did not intend to be mean, but things seemed to just happen without my thinking about them. I guess that I felt that I had to perform out-of-the-ordinary stunts to attract the attention that I lacked in my childhood. Maybe I could be called a delinquent but I had to fight back to maintain my rights. I guess that this behavior was brought about by a need, a lack of something in my life. What was that need?

Whenever I felt that I needed to prove myself, the results were often disastrous (whippings, scoldings, and so on).

Dandy, a race driver, finally came into my life. He had his race cars and shops just a stone's throw from my Mom's home. Each day I would go to see Dandy and ask him if I could sweep the garage floors or clean the inside and outside of his race cars. I wasn't afraid of work. He was very kind to me and paid me for working for him and doing whatever he wanted me to do. My fingers got a little sticky and I began to take an item or two home with me. First it was a pair of pliers, then a wrench, then another pair of pliers, then a screwdriver, and so it went for several days.

"Timmy, I don't want you to work for me anymore and I don't want you to be around here," said Dandy very sternly one morning.

"Why not, Dandy?" I asked. I really was surprised and shocked because Dandy had been one person who I thought cared for me because he talked to me, kidded with me, and paid me for the work I had done.

"I don't want anyone working for me who steals my property." Dandy's voice was quiet and kind, but firm, and I knew that he meant what he said.

"I didn't steal *nothing*," I replied quickly. (I should have used the word *anything*.)

"Timmy, I think a great deal of you and I like to have you around. But you must be a good boy and be honest with me if you want me to be your friend. So you go home now, and when you bring back all of the tools that you have taken from me and you promise never to take anything that is not yours again, then you and I will talk as men and go on from there." Dandy was very nice—I liked him.

Well, I went home and sat down for a while. I couldn't take those tools back and face Dandy. But he was so nice to me I just had to do what he wanted me to do. No, I wouldn't go back. I jumped on my bed and rolled and rolled, trying to decide what to do. About two hours later I went back to the garage with a big paper sack full of tools that belonged to Dandy. I never said a word when I handed the bag to Dandy. I was very sorry inside of me, and I was afraid to look up into his eyes. I handed the sack to him with my head down—way down.

"All right, Timmy," Dandy said softly, "you can still work for me, and I will trust you, but you must promise me that you will never take anything that does not belong to you, promise?"

"Yes, I promise," I replied sheepishly.

Dandy made me understand the wrongness of stealing while at the same time teaching me a lesson for the future. He made me return the stolen goods and told me what I had to do to stay in the good graces of one who had shown me attention and concern. What a guy!

I still want attention and I am going to get it! What a feeling that is, but I guess it is not an uncommon feeling.

Where is Mr. Campbell?

I'm getting sleepy and I have just had my lunch so I guess I will snooze a little.

Permit me to interrupt for a short time while Timmy sleeps.

Children need to feel that they are wanted—don't all of us feel that need? We have many needs that have always been basic to activity, which in turn is synonymous with living. An embryo depends upon its surroundings for sustenance. At birth a child, if normal, breathes, sleeps, and eliminates. There seems to be an eternal debate (with never an exact decision) over what time in the life process each child learns pain, thirst, hunger, laughter, and other needs. Of course, many well-scholared students have given us their ideas in generalities.

In order to satisfy the needs of an infant, he should be active to grow physically as well as intellectually. What kind of activities are we talking about? Is the activity enclosed in a package of motor, muscular, or brain cells? Have we forgotten the idea of activation in order to grow and satisfy needs? If so, where does the child get them—from siblings, peers, parents, or others? Usually the mother or caretaker provides warmth and affection, by holding the child close against the elder's body. This contact tends to create a feeling of security from which growth results.

future, after which we will sit down and talk about them?" she asked insistently.

"Okay," I stammered. "I'll do that, and I will let you know within a couple of days when I am ready to go to see them. But will you go with me the first time?"

"Surely, I will be glad to take you to them, introduce them to you, and stay in their room and watch you and them." Her sweet voice melted my resistance and quieted my fears.

I had been told that one of the patients had been thrown through the windshield of a car, and that he had landed headfirst on rocky ground, leaving a deep hole where his head came to rest, with his feet in the air. He was a young man of approximately twenty-six years of age. He was the father of two children and had been out driving his car wildly after a bitter fight with his wife.

Then a wild but *incorrect* story was told to me about the other person (Timmy told you the correct story in the first chapter).

She said, "There is a lad of eleven years in a room up the hall who was riding his bicycle alongside a buddy on his bicycle, and a drunk driver in a light delivery truck came over the curbing and struck both boys, killing one instantly and knocking the other one into unconsciousness. It appears that he will always be a vegetable."

This accident had happened about six months before. Conditions were still considered unfavorable for both of these patients.

My heart melts and my tear glands generally respond when I see young people or kids hurt, either physically or emotionally.

I sat in my wheelchair and meditated all afternoon after the staff member left my room. I even fought the sleeping and pain pills at night while I thought of who and what I was going to see. I read the Bible and prayed about the upcoming confrontation. Why me? Why was I asked to see these young people? Yes, I had had some experience and responsibility in rehabilitation, but most of it had been with older people in another nursing home. Why was I led through all of my pain and suffering to this place, to meet people who were worse off than I?

This is a basic security that may be carried on into the future, as security tends to give a child an opportunity to face the world and adjust to our ever-changing social environment.

A study by Harlowe indicated that a baby monkey that had been deprived of a mother's love was mentally affected. If the baby monkey was left alone for a long period of time it tended to become withdrawn, with death as a final result in some cases.

Children also need to feel that they are wanted—don't we all feel that need? Lack of this love may tend to lead the child to be aggressive and sullen and not generally accepted by his peer group. Parents who bring a child into this world should consider the child in its growing process. A child may respond to its learning process. So, if a child is nagged at continually, then isn't it almost conclusive that the child learns this condition and accepts it as a way of life (and so accepts it in his "re-activity vocabulary")?

What is re-activity vocabulary? You know what the word *vocabulary* means: Webster listed many definitions but I like to use the following one: "an aggregate or range of things, qualities, or techniques that form the basis of a means of expression. . . ."

Therefore, our re-activity vocabulary is the action station in our brain that tells us what to do, based on the theory we have learned while in contact with our environment. We tend to put in a corner what we see and hear and smell and feel. What corner am I talking about? This corner is in the brain, and we tend to use the basics stored there when we feel that it is appropriate to do so. When we are presented with a problem we lean back on this corner and react accordingly. So we learn to give affection and love and attention as we have received it—we begin to use our re-activity vocabulary.

What is Timmy wanting? He is lonesome and unable to use either his bones or his voice box—what a situation to be in. Sometimes, when you are feeling depressed about some ailment, think about Timmy, will you? Are you as bad off as he is? This is Timmy—no talking, no walking, no movement at all; no eating of solid foods; no drinking out of a glass; no relating when pain is present; no expressing when the need for elimination is present, NO lots of things. Pretty rough, I'd say.

On top of all of these physical problems, Timmy lacks something that deserted him when he was just a small child. Where was the love and the affection and the attention for Timmy? He tried to get along by sulking, being in trouble continually, being stubborn, and doing things to gain attention. For example, Timmy slept in his everyday clothes often. He wore these clothes until he felt that they were to be discarded—not washed—so he sometimes threw them into the stove to burn. Occasionally he would wear a pair of socks for weeks and then destroy them. When he cut some pieces of furniture and slashed carpets he finally got attention, but only temporarily. He got attention, period, but apparently not the love that he wanted and needed.

Why do parents bring children into the world if they do not want to care for and love them? There are many ways in our modern society by which people can avoid conception, so unneeded babies need not be a common thing. If we are not ready to give love and affection, plus a building background and a good re-activity vocabulary, then let's be alert and avoid procreation. Let's not bring someone into our lives—our own child—unless we are ready to help him to adjust to our environment and society. And I mean we must *help* him, so that when we are gone he can say, "I'm glad that my folks helped me to be able to adjust in life before it was too late."

As I study the background of Timmy's life I hesitate to arrive at conclusions because I do not know all of his home life, and I certainly do not want to criticize Timmy's parents, because each parent has his or her own way of raising children. However, I will comment on some of my feelings about Timmy.

Timmy evidently was mildly hyperactive. Many of his problems seem related to a daytime absence of both mother and father in the home, producing an emotional overlay that was used with little motivation or reinforcement. Timmy had difficulties in relating to anyone he wanted to look to for understanding. He found it difficult to control himself. It appeared that he had trouble in handling his impulses and, thus derived, he received little satisfaction from his environment in a wholesome way.

Don't you feel that Timmy still needs love and attention? How will he get these?

I have spoken of love and affection as two different words. Maybe you consider them as being synonymous, but when I read a dictionary I find two different connotations.

> LOVE: a deep devotion for another person or persons; to conceive a strong and passionate feeling for someone or something; the benevolence and mercifulness of God toward mankind.
>
> AFFECTION: fond attachment; an emotion or feeling; a kind feeling—usually distinguished from love.

So, to me, love is a deeper feeling than affection. But as we plod along in life we need both of them. In what order? Not necessarily in any order. Let us not worry about which comes first, but rather concern ourselves that both are needed in our lives for proper adjustment within our environment.

Concern, love, affection, attention, the creation of a feeling of belongingness, a religious atmosphere and concern, cooperation with medical science and therapy. Are these meaningless words and phrases? No, these are needs that are of my concern in working with Timmy. Read on, you will recognize them, I hope.

6

MIRACLES

Timmy knows that he is getting better by degrees, I'm sure, but he is unable to balance the good against the bad, so please permit me to tell you of great things.

When I studied history in high school, I admired most of my teachers even though I did not admire the way that they taught the course. I could never understand what difference it would ever make whether or not Columbus discovered the West Indies in 1492 or 1491 or 1493. I figured that if I knew he had discovered these islands in the latter part of the fifteenth century then that was good enough. I guess that I was not right, because I had difficulty in passing the history courses—just average grades. So I am not going to bother you with many dates in this book. I will mention a few for purposes of record because so many things happened during the course of a *single* year instead of during the course of *many* years.

September 23, 1976

"Is Timmy here?" I asked.

"I know that voice," said Timmy inaudibly. I'll let Timmy tell you about our meeting.

Tears spring quickly to my eyes as I recognize Mr. Campbell. He's back. He's back! He's back! I'm choking inside because I'm so happy. Oh, I wish that I could talk and tell Mr. Campbell how glad I am that he is back to see me. I'm so glad to see him.

"How are things going, my friend?" he asks me. I smile.

"How are you, Mr. Campbell? Is your leg okay? Gee, I hope that you are fine. I've missed you so much." These words were not heard by anyone but I'm sure he knows that I'm so happy. Our one-sided conversation today was so wonderful. I had a marvelous time.

This was the first time that I had visited Timmy since the previous April, when I left the nursing home to go home to recuperate. His appearance was practically the same. Those wild orbiting eyes were still shooting in all directions without co-ordination. His physical condition appeared to be about the same—still no motion. I think that he recognized my voice because he responded immediately when I asked him to close his eyes if he heard my voice—he closed his eyelids and reopened them immediately. He complied both times that I asked him to do so. My visit today was about an hour long, and I felt encouraged with his correct responses and the fact that he remembered me after several months of absence.

"Timmy, if you know who I am, please smile," I asked after I kissed him on the forehead. He responded accurately. His smile is an overextension of the already-open mouth.

About one month after my first visit in September I noticed some movement of his head, very slight, and of two fingers of his right hand, ever so little.

I planned to visit Florida for a few weeks in November and December, so I started to lay plans with Timmy by telling him at least three times before I was to leave that I would be going to Florida for about five weeks. He frowned each time I told him of my future plans.

After the winter season was finally over, and I was able to get outside regularly back home in Pennsylvania, I was literally pushed into going to visit friends in two nursing homes. It was on March 7, 1977, that I was led to visit Timmy and set up a weekly schedule to see him.

Seeing people only once a week really is not enough to help those who need many things. I am hoping that time will permit me to visit Timmy and others oftener than weekly. They need visitation, conversation, and expression of concern for them.

On March 18, 1977, I noticed slight movement of Timmy's facial features. On this day I prayed with Timmy for the first time. Now I feel so guilty. Why didn't I pray with Timmy before? Today was also the first time that I read some verses from the Bible in his presence. Why didn't I read from the Bible before? Am I alone in this failure to talk about Jesus to other people? Have you ever hesitated to mention the Bible to other people? Why? I have asked myself this question many times but seem to have no good answer. But now I have started to converse with Timmy about Jesus and I feel much better. I asked Timmy if he knew who Jesus was and he responded with a smile.

"Timmy, if you know who Jesus was will you please close your eyes?" I asked as I entered his room a week later. I wanted to see if he remembered what I had told him, and if I would get an affirmative response. He closed his eyelids almost immediately and just as quickly reopened them.

I worked some with the fingers on his right hand—there was no movement of the fingers of his left.

The New Testament seemed to be the best place to start reading the Bible to Timmy, so I started with the book of Matthew. After this reading and a short prayer, I fed him some ice cream from a small cup. He is crazy about ice cream, and so am I. Every time I fed him ice cream I would get hungry for some, and would hit the freezer compartment of our refrigerator at home that evening—no *will* power, or is it *won't* power?

Each day that I fed Timmy ice cream he choked or coughed with each swallow. We started with getting him to eat about three-quarters of a cup of that good stuff. Soon he wanted all of it and he seemed to try to move when I told him that there was more if he wanted it.

A miracle happened five weeks after I started to read the Bible to Timmy. On this particular day I did not say "Hi, Timmy, do you know who this is?" Instead I walked into his room and, because he was lying on his back, he was unable to see me (you see, he is not able to raise his head). When he heard my footsteps he became excited and smiled.

But you ask, "What was the miracle?"

As I have mentioned several times, his roving eyes were always dancing wildly. This condition bothered me. I was sure that it was bothersome to him and perhaps kept him from focusing properly. I'm not knowledgeable of much of medicine, although I've taken quite a lot and have had several operations, so I draw my own conclusions.

A MIRACLE! Today both eyes were still—the eyeballs were not chasing each other. Yes, I believe that this was a miracle. How else can you explain the situation?

Things kept happening today. Timmy moved his right arm some and one finger moved a little. He tried to talk with me because I heard air movements coming from his throat. Sure, I agree that therapy has helped Timmy but I sincerely believe that Jesus is working with this lad.

He was very alert and responsive today, and this made me very happy. We prayed together, holding hands as best we could. We had read a chapter from Matthew before we prayed.

Timmy did not cough very much today when I fed him the ice cream—an improvement. So I'm sure you will understand when I say that I went home today on "cloud nine."

"Hi, Timmy, this is Mr. Campbell, how's my big young man today?" I asked as I entered his room.

When Timmy starts to smile after I have been in his room for a short time, generally he wants me to notice something. Today he smiled and then proceeded to move his right hand a little, his right arm moved some also, then he smiled and closed his eyelids for a second.

Today I taught Timmy to wink with his right eye.

"Timmy, when you see someone you like will you wink at them?" I asked. "I suppose that it will be easier for you to wink with your right eye. Oh, by the way, do you know which one is your right eye?" He closed his right eyelid. How about that?

"Also, Timmy, when you want to thank someone for doing you a favor then you should wink at them. Okay?" He winked again.

I use several types of approaches at different times when I enter his room for a visit.

When I walk into his room and do not say a word, he will frown at first and will then smile excitedly. He may even try to utter a sound.

Or I will say, "Is this room 502?" He will respond with a smile.

"Hi, my friend," or "Hi, Timmy," are some other things I say when I enter his room. They seem to work, all of them.

After working with his hands and fingers each time, I read a chapter from the Bible and then we pray. Then it is time for ice cream, which he looks forward to with great anticipation, as indicated by a big smile when the words *ice cream* are mentioned.

Sometimes we just sit, and I hold one of his hands as we talk about football, baseball, or some other items of interest. Some information has been given to me regarding some interesting things that happened when he was active, and many times I get a smile when I mention them.

Usually my visits are of an hour or so duration, but he squeezes my hand when I tell him that I am going home. Sometimes he will frown when I say, "I'll see you tomorrow, my friend."

Today was a rough day for both of us. Why? Well, after doing the regular things, I told Timmy that I would be gone for about four weeks to visit some relatives in Indiana, Illinois, and Iowa. He frowned at length. This hurt me emotionally.

Today Timmy was very alert and he winked at me many times. He is beginning to move his head a little from one side to the other—not much, but at least some. Thank the Lord. He tried to tell me something today, I heard air coming from his throat several times.

We are still reading from the book of Matthew—I read one chapter each day that I visit him. Then the feeding of ice cream follows a period of prayer. After I get through with the verbal prayer Timmy lies quietly for several seconds. I wonder what he is thinking about.

He is eating more ice cream now, and is doing better when swallowing it. Little coughing is noticeable. At first, I placed a spoon of ice cream to the rear of his mouth on the left side—I was instructed to do so. Well, you know me, I want to be different. So I began to feed him the ice cream by placing it on the tip of his tongue so he could taste it better. By feeding him this way, after raising his head a little, as if he were in bed, his coughing diminished a great deal. It was interesting to get him to use his tongue when I put the ice cream on the tip of it.

"Timmy, stick your tongue out at me!" I pleaded.

Timmy frowned at first, and then laughed as his tongue came to the front of his mouth—his mouth is always open. After several minutes of trying to get him to stick out his tongue, he finally got it to his front teeth, which is the maximum extension possible for him. But he soon learned to work his tongue in order to push the ice cream back to his throat—that procedure took some pleading.

The routine of these visits has been outlined before, but after our prayer time I will generally say: "I'll be back in a few minutes." Timmy gets excited because he knows that I am going for the ice cream, which is stored in the refrigerator at the local nurses' station. Interesting.

I have told Timmy many times how we happened to meet and become friends. Now he smiles when I repeat the story because I am sure that he recalls my previous tellings of it.

This is the day that I had told Timmy would come. I am going to leave on my trip and be gone about four or five weeks. I had conditioned him to this by telling him about my trip many times. For the first time I saw moisture in his eyes. I hugged and kissed him and departed—very difficult for both of us.

I don't know how long Mr. Campbell has been gone but it sure seems like a long, long time. I miss him so much. I miss the ice cream, too. Oh, yes, I get some ice cream once in a while with my meal but Mr. Campbell feeds me better than anyone else. [Timmy, of course, is talking to himself.] Gee, I hope that he will be back very soon.

Twenty-two days later I walked into Timmy's room and asked, "Hi, Timmy, how's my good friend?"

He recognized my voice immediately and got excited in *his* way. Imagine his recall after several weeks of absence. That was wonderful, indeed.

Timmy's right hand and arm movements were greatly improved, and he showed me a movement of one finger on his left hand—a first. After the Bible reading and prayer, plus the ice cream feeding, I held his hand for over an hour talking about my trip. He was sitting in his wheelchair, dressed in a red shirt, brown shorts, and red socks. I noticed that he moved his head from one side to the other more easily than before. Again, I say, a miracle plus help from therapy.

"What are you trying to do, punch me?" I asked as he moved his right arm quickly.

Timmy laughed and immediately a noise—not just air—came from his throat and mouth. This was a first and another miracle. He used this vocal sound many times while we talked that day. I understand that the speech pathologist, Darlene, had been working very diligently with him trying to get a sound, and now she has succeeded. Now, Darlene, hear me, please get him to talk. I pray for you, Darlene, as you work with Timmy.

One day when Timmy and I were sitting watching a baseball game on the TV, he squeezed my hand many times. We held hands and talked at times about the game.

Each time I visited Timmy I would mention an incident that had happened to him when in school or before that. Timmy's parents and teacher related some interesting things to me. Sometimes he would respond with a laugh and sometimes he would frown. One time I tickled his nose when he laughed and immediately he frowned. He has a very sensitive nose, I guess.

"You can pray to Jesus, Timmy," I told him many times. "You can pray in your mind quietly. Jesus will hear you." After we pray together he will lie quietly for a while—I'm sure that he is praying, too.

In our prayers I not only ask for help for Timmy, but I also thank Jesus for helping him so much so far. I also pray that when Timmy gets well he will bear witness for Jesus the rest of his life.

Repetition can become monotonous, so I will try to avoid falling into that trap. But I will mention improvements as I notice them.

Timmy is working his lips more now and they are coming closer together, though not touching yet. This will happen.

He knows when I enter his room even if I do not say a word. He knows my footsteps.

"Timmy, I am going to wash your face to get some of your lunch off." He gets a kick out of this procedure even though the water is cold.

He is moving his head with better ease and quickness. And to think that when I first saw him he was unable to move his rigid head at all. MIRACLE.

Today when I read that part of the chapter in Matthew about the three-time denial of Christ by Peter, Timmy smiled and made a sound with his throat. RECALL!

Mrs. Beoratt, supervisor of nursing at the home, went into Timmy's room before I did today. I had asked her to do this, and to notice Timmy's reaction when I walked into the room (as against the response when she walked into his room). I then walked into the room. I said nothing, but at once he responded, even before he saw me. This response was the sound from his throat. He also smiled when I entered. Mrs. Beoratt shook her head as she realized that Timmy had recognized my footsteps even though it had been a week since I had visited him.

I worked with his hands and fingers again today. I noticed that his left arm and hand were a little warm—they have been cold. Now I know that it will not be long before he will have movement of this part of his body.

I never fail to hug and kiss Timmy when I get ready to leave. Also, I tell him that I love him. Many times he will wink at me when I say this.

Sometimes, when I fed Timmy ice cream I would whistle; just whistle, no particular tune. Have you ever done this? Today I started to whistle when I entered Timmy's room. He smiled and uttered a sound as he recognized the whistle. He was in wonderful spirits today. He laughed so many times. I tickled his ribs today for the first time to see if I would get any reaction. His body moved slightly and he laughed.

I was somewhat moved and almost scared today when we were praying. Timmy's body shook, even his legs moved for the first time. The Lord is working. MIRACLE!

7

WAS I REALLY MEAN?

Hi! Timmy here! Are you listening? You'd better hear me because I want to share with you more of my childhood days. Ready? Here we go.

First, will you picture me as a slender or tend-to-be skinny kid with lots of pep? I guess that is one of the reasons that I liked to read about Daniel Boone and his vigorous activities (or did reading about him tend to increase my activities?).

I liked to swim with Artie, my stepbrother, in the swimming hole near our house. Many times other kids would join us in racing different lengths; I guess that I won a few times, especially when the kids were not too old. Oh, yes, sometimes we would wade around and swim usually in our underwear but sometimes we would go skinny wading or skinny swimming—I didn't want to go home in wet clothes.

I liked to play dodgeball and baseball in our pasture and backyard. I wonder what position I would play if I ever played baseball again.

Bicycle riding was great fun. I had a red minibike that I rode until I smashed it so badly that it could not be fixed.

I remember that one time I wore out the tires on my bicycle within four days after getting it as a gift. How could I do that? Easy. Just slide the bike with the brakes on many times after pumping the pedals too fast. I thought that it was lots of fun, that is until punishment came along, and then I had to do without a bike for a long time, until I promised to take care of my things better.

Oh, yes, another time I got mad at my bike so I damaged the doggone thing by kicking it and hitting it with a big stick because it just didn't seem to run right. So what did I do? Well, I threw the two-wheeler into the creek back of our house. How would you like to know someone as mean as I?

"Timmy, where are your dirty socks for the wash today?" asked Dad one Monday afternoon after he got home from work. Dad had to do the laundry in the late afternoon or night because he had to work in the daytime and no one else was around to do that chore. He had it rough, I guess, and we kids did not make it much easier for him, especially me.

"Dad, I still have my socks on," I answered quickly.

"How long have you been wearing them this time?" Dad questioned firmly.

"Oh, a couple of weeks, I guess. They have holes in the toes so you might as well throw them away or into the stove to burn," I had done this trick before. However—you guessed right—I took them off right then and gave them to Dad.

Sometimes at night, after Dad had told us to go to bed and Hank and I had remained quiet for a while, I would begin to pester Hank with the result that a fight followed and then the familiar: "Cut out that noise and get to sleep, both of you! And I mean now!"

That was Dad's voice, and we knew he meant business from past experience. "One more noise and I will be right upstairs to get things settled." And Dad meant just what he said.

We usually went to sleep soon after Dad's remarks.

"Time to get up, you two," a seemingly distant voice sounded. I thought that we had just gone to sleep, and that Dad was getting us up too soon.

"Breakfast is ready, so hurry, right now!" Dad yelled.

Well, when I hear something that means *eat*, I'm on my way. I skipped every other step going down the stairs to get some breakfast. Dad would try to fix different things for the morning meal but regardless of what he fixed, I was always hungry. And even now, considering my inability to handle myself, I'm ready to eat when someone mentions food.

"Timmy, save some milk for me, don't be a hog with it," snapped Ginie, my sister. It seemed that I always happened to get to the refrigerator first at mealtime. I would grab the milk carton and drink as much as I could before the others were ready. First come, first served, that's my motto.

After breakfast came the familiar remark, "Now, you kids, get upstairs and brush your teeth before leaving for school." My Dad really thought of the unhappy things to do. Why brush my teeth every day? Why not once a week; that ought to be often enough.

"I ain't got time this morning, Dad," I mumbled, but he heard my answer.

"Get!" was the quick reply.

So I got going. But this morning I did something that I did sometimes when I was sulky and wanted to get attention. Can you guess? Well, I took a tube of toothpaste and put some on my brush—very little, of course. Then I squeezed the tube until at least half of the terrible-tasting stuff had streamed out like ice cream out of the faucet in an ice cream drive-in. The paste was not quite as thick as ice cream, and really not as tasty either.

Saturday was church day, and the whole family attended services. Dad insisted that we go as a family.

"Where are you going now, Timmy?" asked Dad as I started out the front door after getting home from church.

"Across the road, Dad, to climb the trees in the cemetery." I still had my churchgoing clothes on.

"Okay, Timmy, but change your clothes and put on some older ones if you are going to climb trees."

I jumped two steps at a time going up to my bedroom to change my clothes. I hurried because a friend of mine was waiting for me to "get going."

Climbing tall trees was adventuresome and lots of fun. We would race each other to see which one of us would get to the top first. We might get scratches on our arms and legs, but what the heck, it was great fun to sit up in the trees and look out over the farms around us.

I was not always on the go, since I did like to sit down to read once in a while. I liked the book *Herby* because it had a little love in it. Love was something I missed. I also liked to read mystery stories, jokes, and brain twisters. However, reading in school was not as much fun as reading what I wanted to read. Did you ever feel that way? I'll bet that you have.

One day at school I had been really something. I had lost the chance of enjoying the afternoon recess period because I had fought with some kids during the morning recess. I was sent to the supervisor's office. He was nice to me, and tried to explain, so that I would understand, what it meant to be a gentleman and get along with other people. Well, when I got home that afternoon I was very obnoxious—where did that word come from? I slammed the front door after I entered and then proceeded to irritate everyone who was at home. I pouted while the others were enjoying their supper. I did eat something, but I was nasty with my brothers and sisters.

"Timmy, I think that you should go to bed early tonight," Dad suggested.

"Okay, then I won't have to study tonight," I quickly retorted.

"Oh, no, you won't get by with that," shouted Dad. "You study first, and now, because there is to be *no* running around outside tonight."

Well, the studying time was bad enough but why did Dad impose extra restrictions on me by not letting me run around in the pasture and backyard? I had it rough, didn't I? Did you ever have be bossed like that?

Some neighbors came to our home after I had gone to bed, but I was not asleep yet. What did you do when neighbors visited after you had gone to your room for the evening? Well, I did the same thing you did—I got close to the door and listened. In fact, I left my room and went to the top of the stairs and sat there and listened. Now I wish that I had gone to sleep and *not* listened. Here's why.

"I don't know what I am going to do with Timmy," my

Dad said. He continued, "He is so rebellious." What does that word mean?

"When I tell him 'don't,' he *does* it, and when I tell him to *do* something then he *won't*. For example, he won't change his clothes when he should, and he has to be told to do things because he doesn't appear to think for himself. He destroys things at will, without concern for the possible results. He wants attention all of the time." Dad made quite a speech, didn't he? However, Dad failed to mention that I wanted love in addition to attention and punishment.

"Well, he is just an active kid at heart," a lady's sweet voice echoed. "How old is Timmy now?"

"He is eight years old, but he doesn't act that age much of the time. You'd think that he was many years younger." Dad was irritated.

"Oh, he'll outgrow the present problem, just have patience," the lady said sympathetically. "Wouldn't you rather have an active child than one who is sickly?"

"Sure, but what do you do when your child goes to extremes all of the time?" Dad was really in trouble, as was I. But he continued, "He denies doing things when he does them. This is almost a habit with him. He grabs food at the table first, not thinking about the rest of us. He has destroyed some of his play-things. See the cuts in the furniture? He did that."

"Have you ever thought of Timmy's having some psychological tests?" asked a man's voice. "Sometimes those tests reveal characteristics and causes for them, with a possibility of recommendations for help."

Well, I'm not about to take tests, I thought as I walked slowly back to my bedroom—I got enough testing at school. I did remember taking some special tests at school recently but the teachers would not tell me the results. I think that one of the tests was to see how smart or dumb I was. I wonder about the result.

Regardless, a couple of days later found Dad and me on the way to town. After parking the car and entering a small building I was ushered into a small room. I sat down across from a strange man who proceeded to ask me a lot of questions. I did not answer all of the problems because I had never seen anything like them before. Sometimes I wondered who was being tested, the man across the table or me. I'll tell you, man, some of those questions were "crazy." Enough of that!

Shall we go back to my present home at the nursing home? Okay. Someone is walking into my room and I see a faint outline.

"Are you ready for your supper, Timmy?" asks a sweet voice. I am getting able to see a little better now, but only with my right eye.

I respond with a smile and a noise from my throat. I still cannot talk. Will I ever talk, I wonder. I'm really scared.

The nurse squirts the food down my throat with a large syringe. I am so hungry. I swallow all of the food although I wish that I could reject one item—spinach. I hate that green stuff. But what choice do I have? I just lie there and let someone squirt the spinach down my throat. Some of it runs out of the corner of my mouth. What a deal!

Well, the meal ordeal is over and my mouth and lips have been wiped with a tissue that was dipped in cold water, br-r-r. Then I wink at the "chick"—oh, oh.

I am ready to relax and go to sleep. However, I just happened to think of something that occurred at home, before I became like a vegetable, as they say.

I was taught to be modest and to have clothes on all of the time whenever anyone else was around. Of course, I took off my clothes when I got ready for a bath—and, yes, a few times when I went skinny swimming. One night Hank was getting ready to take a bath. He took all of his clothes off and proceeded to walk around our bedroom—Hank and I shared the same bedroom. I had a small desk in my room that I used for studying, and I happened to be trying to study when Hank was getting ready to take a bath (prior to going on a date, I guess). I always had on shorts, even when I slept. You know, I even slept with my socks on (all of this made it easier to be first downstairs in the morning for breakfast).

"Hank, Dad will be mad at you if he sees you naked," I said. "It isn't nice to let someone else see you without any clothes on."

Hank just laughed and hurriedly went into the bathroom. He came out of the bathroom later, and he had on shorts, so the incident was over for that time. But you will never catch me without clothes on at my age, I'll tell you that. But, you know, I am naked a great deal at this nursing home because the nurses have to give me baths and change my clothes. I guess I'm getting used to it, but I have no other choice now, I can't help myself.

Speaking of clothes, I had a few choice ones that I liked to wear to school and to church. I did want to look nice like most of the other kids, especially when I got into the fourth and fifth grades. I remember that one day I wore my best clothes to school for the school picture. I even had on a coat and tie, which many of the other guys did not.

Hey, tomorrow is the day for Mr. Campbell to come to see me and read to me. I hope that he will not forget to feed me some ice cream. Oh, boy. I'm always glad to see him and glad that he stays quite a while and talks to me. Also, I am very glad and proud when he says that he loves me as he hugs me. That is something I have always wanted—to be loved and to have someone pay attention to me. How would you like it if no one loved you? Do you ever want love, attention, and affection shown your way? Sure you do. Even an animal likes affection, so why not human beings?

I don't know how long I have to live but there is one thing that I will always remember. Yes, I was not too crazy about school, and I was punished there once in a while. There were other disappointments in my childhood days, but the thing I will never forget is when Mom left home for good. I cried very much and very often. I really missed my mother's love.

Guess I'll go to sleep. Oh, before I do doze a little, I want to tell you about a very interesting part of my summer days.

"Dad, when are we going to camp this summer?" This was a question that I asked several times in the early part of each summer.

"In about three weeks, son." My Dad was not nearly as excited as I.

The next three weeks dragged slowly by, and we talked about

the church camp several times a day in our home. All of our family attended the camp period of one week's duration. We always had lots of fun there. Why? One main reason was that we kids were given money to spend for ourselves, and this made me feel big.

Then there were lots of kids my own age who liked to play the same games that I did.

But let me tell you that the biggest reason for my extreme interest in this camp period was that we ate at restaurants and drive-ins every day. Boy, that's what I like—eating at different places.

There were hundreds of people at the camp sessions and we had services at least once a day. But, oh, the horror of going to bed at ten o'clock each night. Of course, we made lots of noise after that hour, but as the week wore on we seemed to be ready to go to sleep after being in bed a few minutes. Things and remarks stopped being as funny as they were the first couple of nights. Know what I mean?

I'm tired. I'm going to sleep. Good night! Wish that you were here to say good night to me.

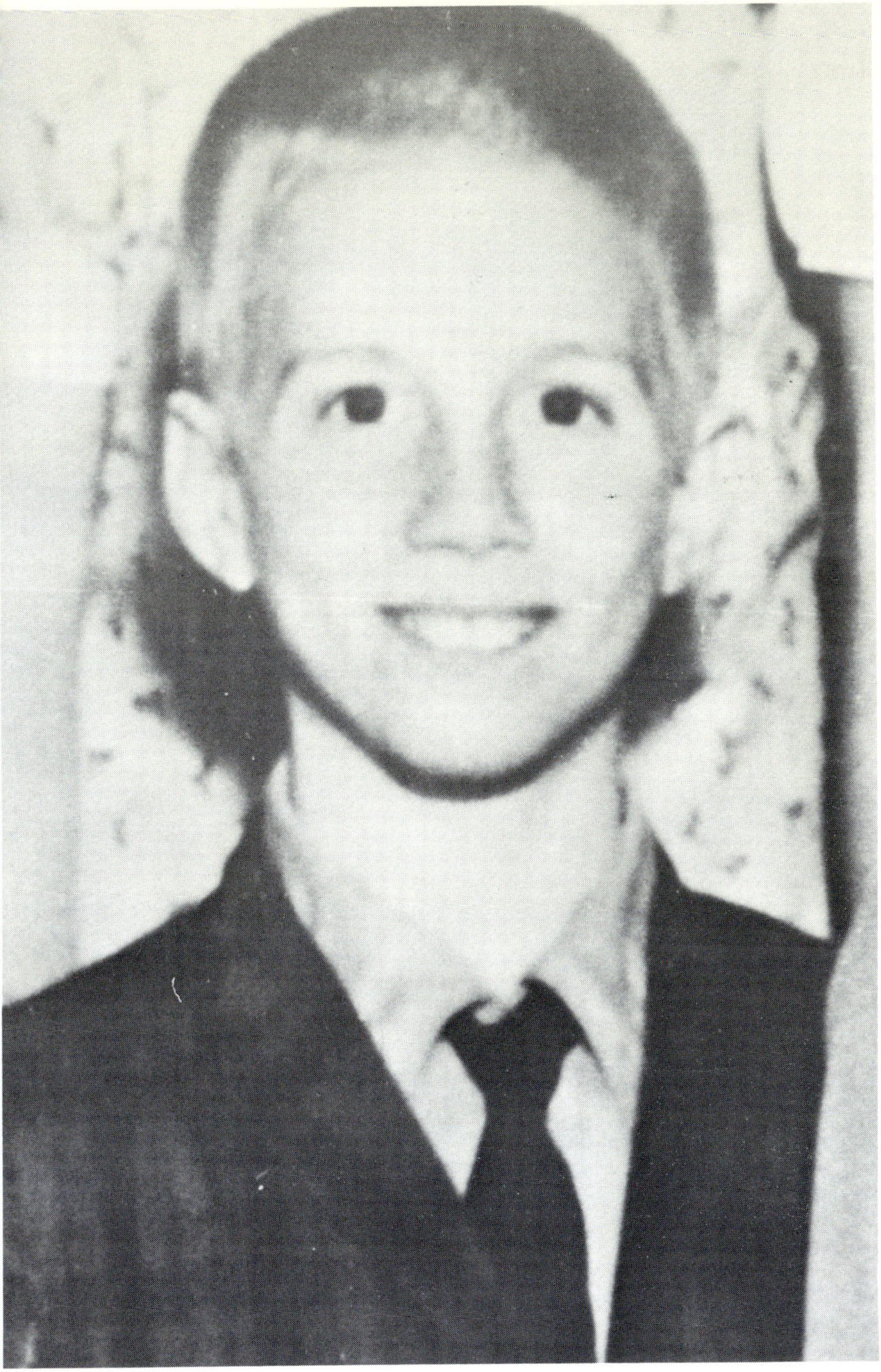

Timmy at the age of ten, two years before the accident

The Colonial Manor Nursing Home in York, Pennsylvania (Timmy's present home)

The author discusses Timmy's progress with D. J. McCormack, administrator of Colonial Manor

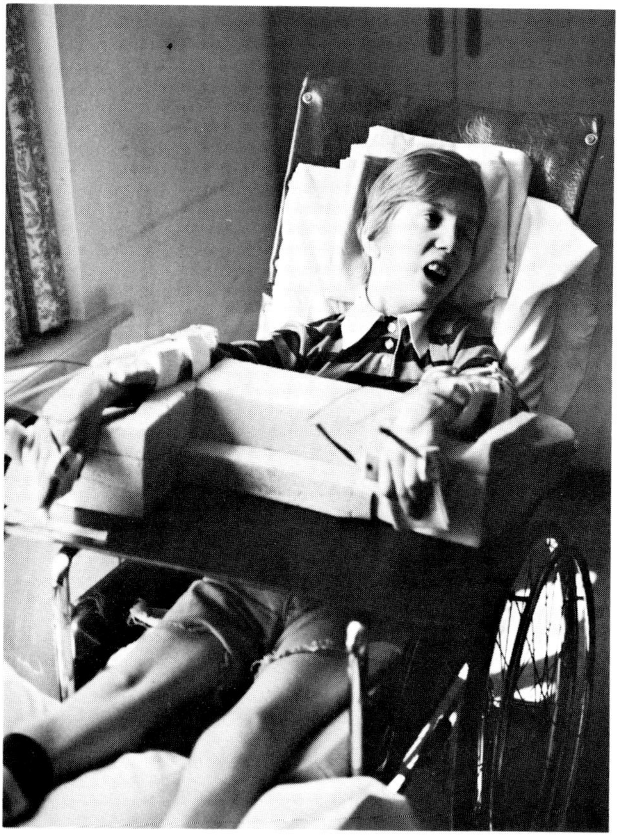

A recent photo of Timmy

)arlene, Colonial Manor's speech pathologist, works with Timmy on a regular basis

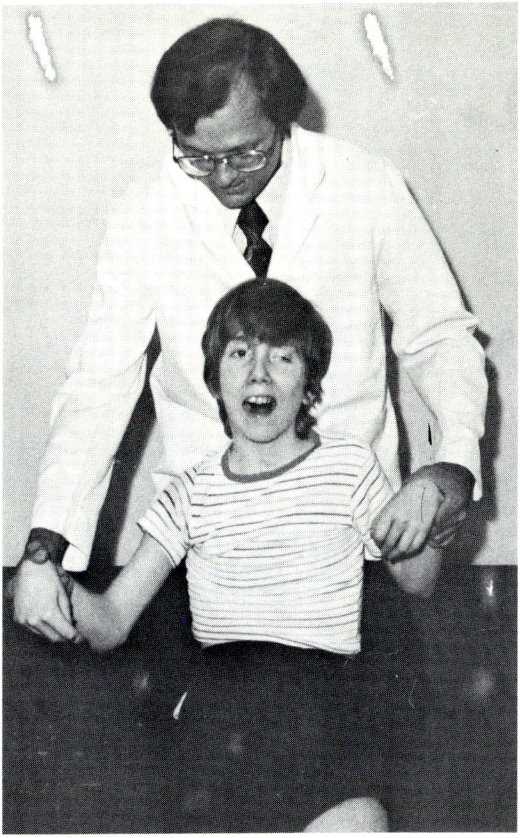

Timmy and Ray, chief occupational therapist at Colonial Manor, work on restoring arm movement

Timmy sometimes becomes the center of attention, as here, with some other residents of Colonial Manor

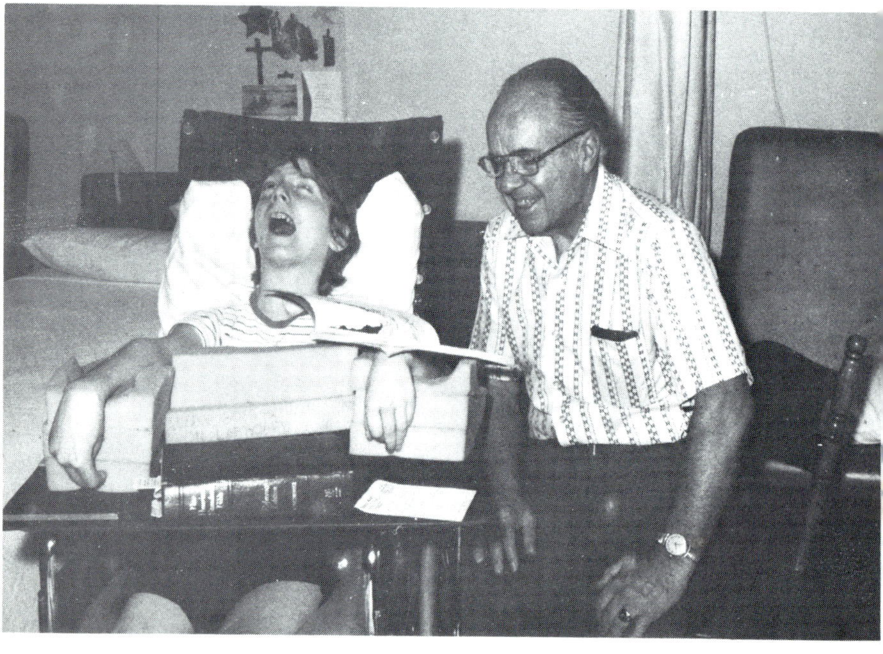

The author reads a favorite story to an attentive Timmy

8

RUNNING AWAY

Shall we allow Timmy to rest and sleep?

While our hero is in his world, will you bear with me as I relate some of the information that I received from talking with Timmy's parents and friends? In all cases I was treated with courtesy and as a friend. There are good people in this world—lots of them.

Religion was a part of Timmy's life. His Dad took the family to church with him regularly and Bible study in the home was a weekly occurrence. Then once a year a summer church camp was promoted, and all of the family really looked forward to the sessions away from home. You remember the details of this camp period, mentioned in the last chapter. Do you think that Timmy might have been a little restless in church and family Bible meetings when he was at a very young age?

"Timmy, will you please stop hitting Alice in front of you?" Mrs. White, a schoolteacher, said, noticing Timmy's misbehavior in class.

Timmy sheepishly lowered his head and tried to hide behind Alice. But Timmy continued to hit Alice when he thought the teacher was not looking in his direction. However, he got caught because he pestered Alice once too often.

"Timmy," said his teacher sternly but softly, "bring your books and pencil up here in front of the room and sit in this armchair."

Unhesitantly, Timmy walked to the front of the room and took his place in the assigned chair. He began to write and draw in his notebook. Timmy did not appear to be embarrassed when he had to sit in front of the rest of the students.

Timmy was reassigned from a female to a male teacher for one of his classes—math—and the report was that he got along better with the male teacher. Was he still disappointed with females because his mother left home when he was very young?

When recess time came, it seemed that Timmy was one of the last picked when sides were chosen; not so much because he was not capable as because he insisted on fighting or kicking other kids—they did not like this. But Timmy would find something to do while the choosing was going on. He seemed to be on the move continually—very energetic.

Let's stay with school activities for a short time, okay? Well, Timmy was very stubborn but no record of corporal punishment was indicated. It appeared that all concerned had tried to use psychology in dealing with him. Timmy would "buck" his teachers almost to the point of challenging them as they requested him to do certain things. For example, Timmy would question and dare anyone to correct him when he disobeyed school rules. Then he would generally take a negative approach in order to gain attention.

One of the teachers felt that maybe Timmy was in a minor state of depression because of the lack of parental love in the home. She tried to give him as much attention as possible by working on his manners and by answering his questions. She also took special time to help Timmy with his studies.

Many times Timmy would not be prepared with homework, and therefore lost some of his recess activities because he had to stay inside and draw, write, or study. It appeared that these restrictions were not bothersome to Timmy.

I looked at one of Timmy's notebooks, which he had at his home. I took it home with me and kept it for some time. Many of the pictures he had drawn were somewhat weird. In fact, Timmy liked to draw and did so many times in preference to listening to social studies instructions and recitations.

One page in his notebook showed two birds in a nest with

their mouths open, evidently waiting for something—food. Another picture on the same page showed two hogs with their mouths open—one of the hogs was in a big box with either water or dirt in it. The other picture was of a strange animal with his mouth open. Do all of these drawings represent an inner feeling of wanting something? The drawing of pictures of this nature, with the mouths open, might tend to reveal an inner feeling of Timmy's; not necessarily a need for food, but a desire for something that he did not have or was not getting.

Many of Timmy's sketches were of cars of the racing variety—good, too. Timmy liked to go to auto races either with his Mom or with his idol, Dandy, the race driver. As with most kids, Timmy would spend some of his time at the races eating hamburgers and drinking milk shakes—as far as his money would stretch. He also loved to spend time in the pits where the race drivers worked on their cars.

Dandy said that Timmy made a pest of himself when he first knew him. He tolerated Timmy only because he felt that something was lacking in his life because he did not want to stay at home much.

"Oh, d——," said Timmy one day, "that was a swear word, and I'm sorry."

"Well, I'll tell you one thing," snapped Dandy quickly, "there will be no more swearing by you, at least when you are in my place. You are too young to use those words and I won't have it. Understand?"

"Yes, Dandy, I'll try to stop using them right now."

Dandy said that he never heard Timmy use another swear word.

"Would you like to have a hamburger or a hot dog?" asked Dandy.

"Oh boy, a hamburger!" exclaimed Timmy. "Am I going with you to get them?"

"Sure thing, Timmy," replied Dandy. So off they went to a drive-in during the lunch hour. This was a frequent happening. Dandy said that Timmy ate as if he was half-starved.

"Here, Dandy, here's something for you," Timmy said as he gave Dandy a centennial jar that he had decorated.

"That is a beautiful thing, Timmy, did you decorate it?"

"Sure did, man," Timmy replied quickly and proudly. "I'm giving it to you because you won a race the other day."

"It sure is beautiful," Dandy said as he smiled at Timmy.

"Now here's something for you, Timmy," Dandy whispered to Timmy. Dandy said that he will never forget the expression of happiness on Timmy's face when he handed a toy sports car to him.

"Thanks for thinking of me, Dandy," said Timmy with tears in his eyes; then he placed his arm around Dandy's waist.

Dandy felt that Timmy was very lonesome some of the time, especially when he was alone in his Mom's home on many week-ends.

Now let us go back to another picture in Timmy's school notebook. It is a sketch of a human hand with *seven* fingers and a thumb. What was he thinking about when he drew it? I laughed as I caught a glimpse of the head of a strange bird with a long beak, protruding at the end of the thumb.

Another item in the notebook showed that Timmy started to print his name but omitted the last two letters because he ran out of space at the side of the paper.

"That is very nice," said one of his parents. "It is beautiful and I like it; did you make it at school?"

"Yes, it took several days," Timmy replied. The item was a large ashtray painted dark green, five and one-half by five and one-half inches, polished.

"Timmy!" said Ginie excitedly, "you know Dad is getting married tonight and I don't want to be home when he and his wife come home because I do not want to cause any trouble. Suppose we hitchhike over to Mom's?"

[Timmy is asleep and is dreaming the following incident, which happened some time ago.]

"That's a long way off and it is late now," I replied.

"Aw, come on, let's go right now." Ginie was ready to leave.

Anyway, off we went down the road, just the two of us. I guess that I was nine or ten then and Ginie was about three years older. After several cars passed us by, a jeep stopped to give us a lift. Many questions were asked of us, like "Where are you going?" and "Are you two running away from home?" We rode several miles before getting out of the jeep.

After two more lifts we knew that we would not get to Mom's home that night. There was a big barn nearby and we were getting tired, so we decided to use the barn for our sleeping quarters for the night and then go on to Mom's the next morning and get some breakfast. It was dark already.

We used a ladder to reach the hayloft, where we went to sleep on some hay. The next thing I knew was that Ginie was punching me in the ribs and saying, "Time to get up."

"I didn't hear any rats or bats last night, did you, Ginie?"

"Nope, and I'm glad I didn't because I would have been scared to death."

When we got to Mom's place no one answered the doorbell. And man, was I hungry—and getting hungrier all of the time. We went next door and the lady there told us that our Mom had moved and did not leave a forwarding address.

"Now what are we going to do?" I muttered, half-crying.

"Well, the only thing to do is to go back to Dad's. We can't stay away another night without anyone knowing where we are." Ginie was getting alarmed.

So we started back to Dad's place. Hitchhiking was not so good that day and we did not get home until late afternoon. We had a small amount of money with us and managed to eat a hamburger during the day.

"Where have you been?" demanded Dad. "Have you been up to some trouble?"

"Ginie and I decided to run away last night because we did not want to cause any trouble between you and our new stepmother. We got a little scared when it got dark, so we crawled up into a hay loft in Mr. Brad's barn. We thought of going farther today but we got hungry and decided to come back home."

"Well, if you ever decide to do anything like that again, let's talk about it first, or at least leave a note so we will not worry about you." Dad was firm in his statements.

We expected some form of punishment but Dad must have been in a good mood this time and he only talked with us.

This "running away" instinct [psychologists, please note] or feeling or urge continued until the summer of 1975. At that time Timmy was eleven years old and he ran away with his older brother, Hank, to stay with his Mom, who lived in another town many miles away.

"Timmy, what do you say that we run away from home here and go to live with Mom?" Hank was disturbed about something.

"No, I'd rather stay here with Ginie and Artie. We have lots of fun playing." Timmy wanted to stay with his Dad and stepmother. Also, Ginie and Artie enjoyed many of the same things that Timmy did.

"Dad told me that I had to get a job, go to school, or join a branch of the armed forces. I don't want to stay here." Hank seemed determined to leave home.

After about a week of coaxing Timmy, Hank told their Dad that they were leaving home. The stepmother offered to drive Hank and Timmy to the home of their Mom, but Hank said that they would rather hitchhike.

The mother accepted them into her home and tried to care for them, even though she worked five nights a week starting about three in the afternoon and not getting home until around midnight. So Timmy was on his own most of the time. This was true even at night, because Hank was dating and thus was gone many evenings.

When the mother came home late at night after work she would wake Timmy and take him to the toilet because he had bed-wetting problems. This act of the mother's helped the situation a great deal. But don't you think that tension aggravated his condition?

It was time to start to school in early September, 1975, and

Timmy boarded the school bus near his mother's home.

"Mom, I met a swell kid at school today. He likes me, and I think that he is really cool," Timmy said excitedly one Monday afternoon when he got home from school.

"Who is he? What's his name?" asked his mother. You see, she did not work on Mondays, so she was home when Timmy arrived.

"Oh, gee, I think that his name is Chuck. And what do you know, he likes things that I do. So tomorrow do you care if I take some of my locks and keys to school and show them to him and maybe give him a couple?" Timmy really was excited. Padlocks and keys were items he played with as a hobby. He would sit for long periods of time, locking and unlocking the locks with the keys.

The mother watched the kids boarding the school bus each morning. She noticed that the boys brushed past the girls and tried to get on first—I suppose that they wanted certain seats.

"Timmy, you should be more courteous in the morning when you get on the school bus. Don't push the girls and crash on ahead of them," she said one morning before Timmy left the house to go to school.

"Okay, Mom, I'll try, but the other boys do it." Timmy conceded.

She watched Timmy wait for the school bus from the living room, and she saw that Timmy would permit the girls to get on the bus ahead of him if they were there by the time he started to get on—latecomers had to take what seats were left. How did you do it when you rode the bus to school? The author had to walk over one mile each way for eight years while in grade school, and then sixteen city blocks while in high school—no buses.

Timmy seemed to be of average intelligence, but tended to hesitate in putting that intelligence to work. He was clever in certain ways, such as suggesting pranks to his brother so that his brother would be the one to get into trouble. For example, Timmy would hand pebbles to Artie and urge him to throw them at passing cars.

The religious aspect of Timmy's life was strong while he lived with his father, but tended to subside some when he lived with his mother. He did not mention religion in the presence of his mother—was he resentful of religion or what?

Timmy's mother felt that he was not a bad kid because he was not in any major trouble, but only misbehaved around the house. He was stubborn, that is true, and he would do things to irritate members of his family in order to get attention.

Timmy was on the go much of the time. He worked in a grocery store while staying with his mother. The rest of his spare time was spent at Dandy's garage, helping with odd jobs. Dandy seemed to have a way with Timmy. He could correct him in such a way that Timmy listened and would come back again and again and not be in a mood of getting even.

There are many more anecdotes that I could mention about Timmy's childhood to twelve years of age. There are many things that you and I did in our childhoods that are never mentioned to anyone, and in many cases are repressed forever.

I'm sure that you realize by this time that Timmy was an active and energetic youth who needed something he was not getting (and I don't mean physical punishment).

Again I go back to the words I have repeated so many times: love, affection, and attention.

Yes, Timmy *was* energetic—until he was struck down by two tons of steel and rubber on four wheels.

9

THINGS ARE HAPPENING

Time passes quickly and I notice that some of the grass in my yard is beginning to turn brown, getting ready for winter. Some of the leaves are beginning to change color—fall is here.

"Is this room 502?" I ask.

A small frown immediately occurs on the face of Timmy. Then there is a broad smile, and then noises that are emitted from his throat indicate that he recognizes me although he is flat on his back in bed.

I am thinking of the time when I asked him, "Timmy, do you know who Jesus is? If you do, please close your eyes." Timmy's eyelids closed immediately, indicating that he was familiar with the name of Jesus. RECALL!

Today was the second time that Timmy's body shook while we were praying. Truly God is working with this child. Timmy moves his head from side to side slowly by himself now, showing a great, but slow, improvement in the past several months. The nurses and aides prepare him somewhat for my visits by reminding him that it is Thursday, the day when Mr. Campbell visits. Timmy responds, I am told, with many loud noises from his throat and movements of his mouth and hands. Now even his left foot moves ever so slightly. The nurses tell me that this action occurs each time that they mention my name.

Yes, I noticed today when I first approached Timmy in the hallway and spoke to him that in his excitement his left foot was moving—it was very noticeable to me.

Sure, therapy is helping Timmy, but I am positive that the Lord is also working with this lad, slowly but surely. But we need prayers—will you pray?

One of the nurses told me that Timmy was very restless last night. You see he is unable to tell anyone if he has pain or is sick somewhere; isn't that terrible? I really feel sorry for him but I try to avoid showing it when I am with him. I told one of the nurses that if at any time in the future, day or night, he got restless and no one at the home was able to quiet him, they were to call me and I would come to see if I might help him. So she wrote down my telephone number on his records and promised that someone would call me as requested.

On this particular day I read the third chapter of Mark, wherein there are many cases of healing by our Master. Timmy closed his eyes when we prayed. Even after we finished with our prayer he kept his eyes closed for a few seconds, then he lay motionless several seconds staring up at the ceiling—I'm sure that Timmy was praying, too. I told him that Jesus loves him and that He was helping him and would continue to help, but that Timmy needed to pray also.

"Timmy, some day Jesus will have you talking. I want you to say 'Jesus loves me' when you start talking," I said repeatedly.

We talked about baseball today and the standings of the major league teams. We tried to guess who might win the play-offs and the World Series. It appeared that the Pittsburgh Pirates were his favorite team, because he reacted more when this team was mentioned.

I worked with his right hand and arm, which he is able to extend to his leg. Then I took his right hand and started to help it back to his chest.

"What are you doing, Timmy, fighting me?" I asked as he stiffened his right arm and showed me his strength to avoid bringing his arm back to his chest. So now when I work with his arms I'll say "fight me" when I try to bring his right arm back to his chest. He laughs and gets quite a kick out of it when it appears that he is winning the battle.

The other day one of the therapy aides at the home took

Timmy out to the York Fair and spent several hours there. He was in his wheelchair. Many of the barkers at various stands gave him balloons and teddy bears, big teddy bears, six in number. I was told that he had a grand time.

Today was fun. A birthday party was held for members of the home who had birthdays in that particular month. The day itself was really Timmy's birthday. I think that someone planned it that way so Timmy would be the guest of honor.

I took Timmy in his wheelchair to a large room, where about twenty-five other residents were sitting—most of them also in wheelchairs. After a period of entertainment by two local belly dancers we had refreshments and music. I fed Timmy pineapple upside-down cake, which he was able to swallow slowly with some choking and coughing. He also got some ice cream and then some punch. He was given the punch with a large syringe. I asked him several times if he had drunk enough of the punch but each time he would make a sound from his throat indicating that he wanted more. So we did not stop the punch until he had consumed a full glass. It helped to wash down the loose crumbs of the cake. All of us had a grand time.

Guess what. After I took Timmy to his room I fed him some more ice cream—rich ice cream, some of that special birthday cake ice cream. And did he raise a fuss when I suggested that he had eaten enough ice cream for this time. I never inquired as to how much supper he ate that evening—I wonder.

Again let me remind you that my regular routine when I visit Timmy is to greet him, call him by his name, and mention my name. In fact, I may just stand and say nothing at first, waiting until I see that he recognizes me by the expression on his face. I work with his fingers, hands, and arms; I read the Bible and then pray; sometimes I read a chapter from a mystery story—he likes the mysteries; then I feed him ice cream and give him some water to drink; then I wash his face with a paper towel dipped in cold water. After this procedure we sit and talk about various things while we hold hands. A hug and a kiss on the forehead or cheek and I say "So long, kid." Do you have any suggestions that I could add to this procedure?

When I mentioned the name of Joe Namath today Timmy got excited. I'm sure that he recalled the name. Then we talked about football for quite some time. Football was the topic of conversation for the next several weeks because the season was upon us. We enjoyed it even as we think of those lady folks at home who do not watch the TV when the football games are on.

The speech pathologist, Darlene, and the occupational therapist, Ray, were very cooperative when I inquired about their efforts and results with Timmy. These two very fine and capable individuals have spent many hours working with Timmy. They have permitted me to watch them work with the residents, especially Timmy. I hope that they do not give up hope. They are young but they really have great patience and talent. Although progress is very, very slow I feel that progress is there. Even a slight change is noticeable as I watch closely during each of my visits. You know, I have always been that way with my car, listening for any little squeak or noise that other people might not notice. So we must have patience, faith, and love.

Do you know how much ice cream Timmy is eating now when I am there? I get a large cereal dish and fill it full, and you should see the expression on his face when I show it to him and ask him if he thinks that he can eat all of it. Of course, you must know by now what kind of reaction I get from him then. I purchase a half-gallon of ice cream, which is kept in the freezer unit at the home with the name "Timmy" on it. It doesn't last too long, either.

Mr. McArt, the supervisor of the nursing home, and Mrs. Beoratt, the supervisor of nursing services, welcome me in their offices upon my requests, and they do not rush me to leave—so I try to be brief. Cooperation has been IT with them. And while I am on the subject of cooperation, let me take time to remind you that cooperation is necessary when so many are involved. That has been an unspoken motto of all who work with Timmy. Even the activities personnel have asked me, "What can we do to help?" So what do I tell them?

"When you go into Timmy's room, don't just say hello but take time to hold his hand or hands for a few seconds to let him know that he is noticed and that someone else cares. Just a few seconds will help."

One of Timmy's roommates was an older man of about eighty-five. One day a lady came into the room to visit this older man. When she walked out she made the following remark: "What a shame."

"Please, lady, you have just set me back about six weeks by saying those three words," I said as I followed her into the hall. "He can hear you and his mind knows pretty well what is going on."

She apologized and promised that she would hold her tongue when around Timmy in the future.

I returned to the room and hugged and made a fuss over Timmy. I stayed about an hour longer than usual, because I was trying to erase the lady's remark from his thoughts.

Whenever you visit a hospital or nursing home, please be careful of your choice of words. Offhand remarks may penetrate the patients' minds, even if you think that they might not understand because their brains are not working as they once did. Wait until you get outside the building to make remarks that you do not want the patient to hear. While you are in the room, please encourage the patients and make them feel that you are there to visit them because you CARE and want to see them. Don't let them feel that you came to see them just because you feel that it was your duty, or feel sorry for them.

When Timmy is in good spirits, as he was today, he appears to understand past experiences when I mention them to him. He reacts with frowns, smiles, noises from his throat, and movements of his right hand. By the way, I was able to move his left hand back and forth about half an inch today—what an improvement. He winked at me many times while I was feeding him ice cream at his bedside. You remember that I taught him to wink with his right eye when he saw someone he liked or when he wanted to thank someone. He was "cute" today in many ways. He seldom coughs when I feed him now, which is quite an improvement. He used to cough with *every* bite. Things are happening—good things!

A favorable response was noticed today, when I mentioned the name of Mr. Harrison, supervisor of the school Timmy had attended. I thought that while I was at it I would also mention the name of one of his favorite schoolteachers, Mrs. White. He smiled and made noises with his throat when both names were mentioned. I hope that those sounds will soon be words. I know that he will talk someday. I know it.

Timmy was a little confused today when he heard other footsteps in addition to mine as I entered his room. When he is confused there is a frown on his forehead, between and just above his eyes.

"Timmy, I'd like for you to meet a Christian friend of mine, Mr. Bent," I said.

"How are you, Timmy? I've heard so many good things about you," said Mr. Bent as he took one of Timmy's hands and then talked with him very softly.

Timmy smiled as Mr. Bent held his hand so I knew that he had accepted Mr. Bent at once. Wasn't that wonderful? Mr. Bent spent about an hour with us and prayed while we three held hands. What a marvelous inspiration.

"Now, Timmy, please show Mr. Bent how strong you are, fight him like you do me," I told Timmy as I indicated to Mr. Bent what he was to do with Timmy's right hand and arm. Timmy really braced his right arm and laughed excessively when he "beat" Mr. Bent in resisting the movement of his right arm. That incident made us feel good.

Now and then I intersperse an extra visit between regular Thursday visits. Well, one Sunday as I sat at home, not in the mood for watching TV or reading, I decided that the thing I should do was to go visiting. So where did I go? You guessed it—to the nursing home where Timmy was.

As usual, both of us were glad to see each other in room 502. I went through the usual routine so Timmy got extra Bible reading, prayer, and ice cream that week. I tickled Timmy's ribs and felt that his clothes were wet.

"What goes here?" I asked. "Was some water spilled on your

clothes during your lunch?" It was about 1:20 P.M., shortly after lunch or dinner time, whatever they call it.

Timmy laughed as I told him that I would ask one of the nurses to come in and change his clothes so he would be more comfortable. One of the aides came in as soon as I asked her to do so.

"I'll change him right away," she said as she started to take off the wet clothes. "Sometimes the urinal laying between his legs spills, with the result of more wet clothes than usual."

"Thank you so much." I looked at the aide as she completed dressing Timmy with dry clothes.

"Okay. You're welcome," the aide replied as she hurried out of the room—to help someone else, I suppose.

"Timmy, don't worry about getting wet, don't be embarrassed with Mr. Campbell. When you got to go, you got to go." That remark caused a noisy laugh from our friend, Timmy.

Mr. Bent visited with Timmy and me again and Timmy reacted favorably when he heard Mr. Bent's voice. He did better than some older folks in recognizing a voice after a week of absence. I think Timmy's recall is wonderful considering his condition.

While kidding Timmy today about some of the pranks that he did when younger, he passed some air and frowned.

"That's okay, buddy, don't worry about it, all of us get into that position once in a while," I said quickly. Timmy then laughed.

Yes, things are happening, and improvements will continue to happen in the life of Timmy. I KNOW THIS!

10

KEEP GOING, TIMMY

I am still unable to talk, except to myself in my mind. If I could talk aloud I would tell Mr. Campbell lots of things. For example, I wish I could tell him that I have difficulty in focusing my right eye. Also, I see only dimly until the object gets fairly close to me, then I can see good (that is, with my right eye). Mr. Campbell seems to have figured out my problems. He shifts cards and other objects from a distance to a closer look for me. Oh, here he comes now.

"Hi, my friend, how are things going today? Everything okay?" Mr. Campbell asks me as I sit in my wheelchair. My head is hanging down almost to the shelf of my wheelchair and saliva is running out of my mouth.

"Help me straighten up, will you, Mr. Campbell?" I am pleading with my facial expressions. "I have been sitting in this position for a long, long time and I am tired." I tried to explain.

"I am going to get a nurse to help put you in a different position so you will be more comfortable," Mr. Campbell was so understanding.

Well, I got straightened up and I feel much better.

"Timmy, you are moving your left arm today. Let me help you. Now let's see how far we can move it toward your left leg," Mr. Campbell was working slowly with my arm.

"We made it, we made it!" shouted Mr. Campbell. The hand had touched my left leg and with his help it was returning to my chest.

"Guess I'll take a nap now that Mr. Campbell has left for today," I was getting sleepy, and already I was very tired.

While Timmy is sleeping I suppose that he is having fond dreams of the good old days.

So you see that I am taking over for a while. Timmy is moving both arms without help. What a great improvement from two years ago. Is that a long time? Sure it is, but there is progress forward not backward, and that is something to be thankful to the gentleman upstairs for.

A piece of cake was part of the surprise for Timmy today. I broke up the large piece into small fragments. He has trouble in swallowing so caution must be used to avoid choking. I showed the first piece to Timmy and told him that it was a piece of cake. I think that he recognized it even before I told him because he got excited immediately. Maybe he smelled it.

"Now Timmy, I am going to place a piece on your teeth instead of on your tongue like I do ice cream, because you have to chew it before you swallow it to avoid choking and coughing as much as possible," I said slowly so he would understand.

I placed a small piece of chocolate cake on some of his teeth on the left side of his mouth. You see, I am trying to get him to use his left side in many areas because that is the side that appears to be the slowest to respond to any treatment.

"Timmy, don't do that, don't bite me," I laughingly remarked as Timmy bit down on my finger lightly when I fed him the second piece of cake. He did not bite hard, but just enough for me to feel it. He laughed for a long time. This trick of his happens at least once or twice whenever I feed him cake. We always laugh and have a good time when this occurs.

Well, he did well and did not choke. First a spoon of ice cream, a piece of cake, then ice cream, then cake, and so on until all of the cake and ice cream were gone. Then he drank a full cup of water.

Sometimes I wash his face when I visit him even before feeding him. One day his face was drawn a little to the left and it scared me because it was so noticeable, at least to me, as I watch for even minute things. Had he suffered a slight stroke on the left side? I soaked a paper towel in cold water and then washed his face to remove some dried lunch around his mouth. I was hoping that this was the reason for his face being a little out of shape. I was so happy when his face went back to its regular shape after I finished the wash job. He winked at me when I finished, although I did use cold water—I guess he is used to it by now.

Artone Smythe, a brother-in-law, visited with me while doing some research about Timmy. We also spent some time with Timmy one day. Timmy kept uttering sounds from his throat while I was busy writing some notes. Finally I had to stop writing and spend time with Timmy. At least he quieted down while we held hands.

Artone and I were permitted to sit in Darlene's office the next day. You will remember that she is the speech pathologist. We listened and watched as she worked with Timmy for about twenty minutes. The session was not too rewarding as Timmy was very tired and he had company, too.

After a nurse's aide took Timmy out of the office, Artone and I sat and talked with Darlene, discussing many things. She decided to have sessions with Timmy shortly after lunch figuring that he would not be so tired at that time of the day. We mentioned the pros and cons of what I was doing and what she was accomplishing—the discussion was very rewarding for us. She appears to be very interested in Timmy.

Timmy listened quietly as I read the Christmas story as related in the second chapter of Matthew.

A week later the story of the shepherds of the Christmas story as told in Luke was enjoyed by Timmy as well as myself.

There has been some question as to the working of Timmy's left eye. One person said that there was no reaction whatsoever and had not been since the accident. Well, dumb me decided to get to work on it.

"Timmy, let's do something different today," I began to explain after being with Timmy for a little while. "Mr. Campbell will not hurt you. Here's what I am going to do. I will cover your right eye with my hand. Don't be afraid. Oh, by the way, which is your right eye?" Timmy closed his right eyelid immediately and as quickly reopened it.

"That's fine," I delightedly said as I placed a cupped hand over his right eye and moved a finger up, down, and sideways in front of his left eye. No response to the stimulus was noticeable. But I am not disheartened. I will try again and again with various objects.

Timmy did not respond when he was showed a group picture of his fourth-grade school class. Then, when I showed him a picture of himself that had been taken from the group picture, he smiled and got excited. Evidently there was too much in the group picture for him to focus properly. I told Darlene about this incident. She said that some pictures she had shown him resulted in the same reaction—the less items in the picture the better the response.

The nurses and aides had decorated a small Christmas tree and placed it on the stand by the head of Timmy's bed. He received many gifts and cards. The people at the nursing home really let him know all of the time that he is part of their life and that he is loved by them.

Timmy, with my help, moved his left arm from his chest to his left leg and then, by himself, brought it back up to his chest. Now both arms are moving with his control whereas several months ago neither arm was moving up and down—very rigid. Do you believe in miracles? I do; I have seen them happen with Timmy. Thank you, Jesus. Timmy is able to stiffen his left arm almost as much as his right arm—this is something. His fingers are still stiff and immovable, except two on his right hand. I'm really thankful so far.

After working with his left eye today, I thought that his eyeball moved ever so slightly to the left but not up or down. Am I imagining or hoping? But both eyes seemed to coordinate a little for the first time.

Some of Timmy's family were with his Dad in his room tonight as I entered. I had asked them to meet me at 7:00 P.M. They were showed what Timmy could do physically, because I wanted them to help him whenever they visited him.

I walked down the hallway when the family left, and they said that they were so glad to see the progress Timmy was making. Timmy was also glad to see them as indicated by his reactions. I hope that the family will visit Timmy often.

"Timmy, I am not going to give you drinking water with the big tube or syringe today—I am not going to shoot it down your throat." Guess what—he smiled. "We are going to use a cup." I was talking like this as I poured some ice water into a paper cup, then I showed him the cup.

"Now close your lips as much as you can and drink some of this water. You are going to have to swallow so the water will go down," I said as I placed the cup to his lips. This procedure was accomplished with some difficulty. He coughed with every swallow. But I was not going to give up because I was sure that Timmy would rather drink out of a cup than from a syringe.

"Timmy, I am going to keep doing this. You are going to learn to drink from a cup, and you will do so in the future when I am here. The water tastes so much better going over your tongue," I confidently said. "Do you want some more?" I asked when over half of the cup of water was gone. Timmy grunted as he does when he wants more or does not want a person to stop what he or she is doing. Would you believe it; he drank a full cup of water even though he coughed with every swallow.

After I left Timmy's room today I stopped at the nurses' office, which is just a few steps from his room. I advised the personnel of the experiment with drinking from a cup, and asked them to do the same in the future.

"Timmy, now start swallowing. I want you to swallow two or three times without stopping," I said today as I placed the cup of water to his lips. What do you know, he coughed less, even when taking several swallows at one time. I guess the air was not interfering with each swallow. I complimented Timmy on his ability to drink from a cup—he smiled and winked at me. I always compliment him whenever he accomplishes anything—this is a must as a conditioner as well as a show of caring.

Timmy reacted with a facial expression of excitement when a nurse reported to me that someone had made ice cream with snow and cream and sugar the other day. "And did he like it," she said. Remember when we were kids we used to do this—snow with good cream, vanilla, and sugar? H-mmmm, good.

Timmy has a TV set but it is across the room from his bed, which makes for poor vision for him. So today I asked Mr. McArt, the supervisor, if it would be possible to have a small portable set placed near his bed, hanging from either the ceiling or the wall, in order for it to be moved and placed in positions for Timmy to see and follow even while he is in bed. I believe that the movement of the pictures themselves, as well as the movement of the set, a few times a day might improve his vision. It would at least tend to exercise his eyes and maybe help his left eye also. Mr. McArt listened and said that there might be a problem in bringing the cable over to the other side of the room, but he promised to check it out and let me know.

Today I was sitting with Timmy, who was in his wheelchair. I was holding his hands while gearing my attention to the program on TV. After a while I glanced toward Timmy and saw that he was staring at me. As our eyes met he winked at me twice—bless him.

Dr. Marnie was asked about the possibility of having a Home Bound teacher help Timmy with some school work. I felt that Timmy's brain, which is now functioning some, should not be given a chance to regress or degenerate. We must keep it alive. However, it was indicated that a person with proper expertise was not available in our community. But he added that if I could come up with something substantial that would benefit Timmy he would listen. I also recommended that an EEG be given in the near future to help us in knowing how much brain damage exists.

Sure, it has been over two years since that awful day when

the terrible accident happened to Timmy, but don't you feel that there has been progress?

I feel that the combination of science, faith, and love have produced miraculous results. Let us also add one of the most important items in this case—a belief that our Lord works miracles and that He is working with Timmy.

Prayer is helping greatly—I know this.

☙ 11 ❧

WE'RE MOVING

We need to keep Timmy's brain cells alive and functioning. We do not dare to let them fall asleep.

Many authorities listened to my plea for some added schooling for Timmy. But most of them seemed to feel that Timmy was not "ripe" for this type of program yet and that no one with special abilities was available.

"Why don't you try to work with Timmy?" asked Darlene. "You seem to get him to respond better than anyone else."

"But that would take four or five days a week to do an effective job," I hesitantly but weakly replied. But then I thought that I would never have a good excuse if someone asked me why I couldn't spend that much time with Timmy. So I agreed to try to help Timmy in an educational way.

Darlene recommended that I spend about fifteen minutes a day in a structured lesson with flash cards containing monosyllabic pictures and words.

So Timmy was conditioned for a few days by my telling him that we were going to have a little school with each other. He responded favorably with a smile each time that I told him of our plan.

The first day of structured time with the cards went something like this:

"Now, my friend, I'm going to show you some pictures and explain them to you. Then I will spell the name of that object each time. I will show you the spelling as I repeat it." I was hoping that the response would be good even on that first day.

But Timmy decided this first day that he was not going to cooperate with me. He kept his head turned away from me and continually looked at the ceiling. After some pleading I decided to get firm with Timmy.

"Timmy, Mr. Campbell drives several miles to come in to see you and to be with you. Now, if you are going to be stubborn then I will walk out that door and when you do turn your head this way you will not see me." I was speaking with a firm but not nasty voice. "Is that what you want?"

Very slowly his head moved in my direction and I kept silent until he had moved his head all the way across the headrest on the wheelchair. He smiled and then winked at me. Moisture gathered in my eyes. I really felt sorry for him but I felt that firmness was necessary.

We looked at about twenty cards and I explained what they were and also spelled each one. He looked at the pictures but tended to let his eyes stray when I spelled the words. He did not respond too well, but we will keep at it.

After our regular routine, I stood up. Immediately Timmy began to cry—this was the first time that I had heard this particular sound, which was quite different than the regular sound he had been making for several months. An aide came into the room hurriedly.

"What's the matter, Timmy?" she asked as she kissed him on the cheek.

"I think that he is afraid that I will go and not come back because we had quite a talk today. But I had to get firm." I was choking a little as I replied.

Timmy was then placed in his bed. The nurse's aide thought that he was getting tired because he had been sitting in the wheelchair for several hours.

"I'll see you tomorrow," I said as I started to leave room 502. Timmy stopped crying immediately.

And some people try to tell me that his brain is not functioning? Maybe not 100 percent, but normal in many ways.

Timmy now uses a crying sound when he is uncomfortable or has an ache somewhere, or when perhaps he is tired.

He winks at me when I straighten him in his wheelchair.

Imagine how you would feel if you sat in one position for hours as he does. He is unable to move any part of his body to shift positions. The crying sound can be heard in the hall and down to the nurses' station. This sound is quite different than other sounds he makes, and the sound that Darlene taught him.

Ensuing days have been a little encouraging. He recognizes some of the pictures on the flash cards. When he does not see a familiar picture he sometimes frowns, but smiles when he sees one that is familiar. We try to point out the color, size, description, and sometimes a little story about each one of the pictures. He really responds quickly and noisily when I show him a card with a picture of a racing car on it.

"Timmy, would you like to go with Mr. Campbell to the kitchen to get a dish and a spoon for your ice cream?" I ask.

What kind of a response do you think I get? You guessed it, a smile and a sound from his throat. He really gets excited.

Now he reacts excitedly whenever I ask, "Timmy, do you want to go with Mr. Campbell to the kitchen?" No need to mention spoon, dish, or ice cream—he knows. Or I may just ask, "Timmy, shall we take a walk?" The response is similar.

Generally, he holds the spoon between his fingers on the way back to his room, while the dish rests on the large board on his wheelchair on which his hands rest.

I am amazed at some of Timmy's reactions, which differ at times. For example, we prayed today after reading a passage from the book of John. Soon after I started to pray Timmy started to talk (in his way), and kept talking until I finished praying Was he praying also? I think so.

One day I was not in a particular hurry to get home for supper so I stayed with Timmy longer than usual. While I talked with him he would look up at the ceiling most of the time. I wonder, what was he thinking about? Someday he will tell me, I'm sure. When I ran out of things to talk about he was very quiet for a few minutes. He looked over at me after turning his head slowly and winked at me—I returned the wink. Then he emitted his regular sound for several minutes, appearing relaxed and happy.

I told you before that hope for the sight of his left eye was negative, but that I was going to keep working and hoping and praying.

"Timmy, again I am going to cover your right eye. I won't hurt you, you know that, don't you?" I opened a drawer in his night stand and took out a toy drag racer. I held it in front of his left eye, and what do you think, he reacted excitedly—the same way that he does when he recognizes things or people. Yes, we're moving right along. After months of working and praying he is seeing with his left eye! A MIRACLE!

I have wondered how near an object must be to Timmy's eyes before he can focus properly. Today I took several large flash cards, one at a time, and started at the end of his bed and kept moving them closer to his eyes. In each case he reacted when the card was about two feet from his right eye and about ten inches from his left eye.

Poor guy, I feel so sorry for him in many ways. The braces on his hands must be painful much of the time. I know that they hurt him because he frowns at times and sometimes cries.

The other day he started to cry and kept it up for a few minutes, so I placed my arm around him and held him for a while. Soon he stopped crying. However, he kept moving his arms in a nervous jerky mannerism.

Now I am starting to work with his legs. He has responded ever so little when I ask him to move his right foot or his left foot. I notice that he works hard to satisfy my requests because I see his arms twitch and a frown on his face when he tries to move his legs or feet.

"Timmy, as soon as the weather warms up, possibly within a few days, Mr. Campbell will take you outside for a walk. Would you like that?" I expected some reaction.

Timmy smiled and winked.

12

LOVE-PRAYER-CARING

Where do we go from here?

Are we on the right track?

Should we set the throttle on "full speed ahead"?

Now wait a minute, let us sit down and relax and meditate about the future. Help me. You *can* pray, can't you? You *will* pray, won't you? Let us get serious. I'm not going to give up.

Remember, Timmy was given excellent medical and nursing care while he was in the hospital but he was released to the nursing home with the observation that he was comatose, without response to external environment (as with all comatose patients).

What a future for Timmy. The future program was already planned for him. Or was it? If so, whose pattern was being followed? Whose pattern or program must we use?

Is Timmy still a vegetable as he was many months ago? No, he is not! Some may refer to him as in a vegetable state because of his present condition. But I have seen great improvement in his reactions. Oh, if only he could tell me what he is thinking and what he is desiring. He will, I know he will, before too long! All of this is in the pattern set up by one mightier than we.

Timmy is destined to be the patient of a skilled nursing facility for the remainder of his life—according to the "experts." They once said that he had reached the plateau; that the potential for Timmy had been attained as far as rehabilitation was concerned. This admission was made several months ago, but now they admit that there is some hope for improvement in nonverbal communication. What a future. *But,* I don't feel that way. A year after the "expert" opinions were written, so much improvement has been noted in many ways.

WOW! I received a severe shock today as I reviewed some records. Having studied some psychology, I read many times that brain stem damage could result in indefinite coma with little or no repair of the brain stem. Well, today, I saw "Brain Stem Contusion" on Timmy's file. Oh, no. I was ready to give up. But why should I stop now? I'll tell you why I shouldn't—improvements have been noticed since that phrase was put on his records. He is not in a coma, far from that. I wonder what I would have done if I had seen that remark before I saw Timmy, I wonder?

I am sure that all medical professionals must have faith in their ability to do the one or the other thing, which is very, very important. How many people of the medical profession have faith in our Lord? I do not have any statistics to answer that question. I can only hope and pray that surgical hands and educated brains rely on a power mightier than those of humans.

So let us assume that there is now a break between the medical profession and the faith we must have in the future healing of Timmy. Certainly if skilled people had not worked with Timmy at the hospital, in the ambulance, and at the nursing home, Timmy would not be alive today—he was "dead" on three different occasions shortly after the accident. Instruments, brains, skilled hands, and medical science were used to keep him alive. So we give you heaps and heaps of credit—all of you—in the medical and therapeutic fields.

So what is left to do? We want those in the medical and skilled fields to continue helping Timmy. But, in addition, we know that we must use prayer, love, and faith with this young lad, our hero.

What is prayer? Some have said that prayer is the soul's sincere desire, expressed or unexpressed. . . . Some have said that we dream and hope through prayer. We need to find the source of fulfillment in this uncertain world through the use of prayer.

In Mark, chapter 11, verse 24, we find "Therefore I say to you, all things for which you pray and ask, believe that you have received them, and they shall be *granted* you."

Then let us back up a little, and return to the first book of the New Testament. Matthew refers to the statement made by Jesus, "Again I say to you, that if two of you agree on earth about anything that they may ask, it shall be done for them by My Father who is in Heaven." (Matthew 18:19)

What do we do now? Ask Jesus for help with Timmy and then sit in a comfortable chair in front of a lighted fireplace and, when no results are realized, immediately decide that smoke has gone up the chimney into the air? You had better not pray and think in this manner. Why do I say this? Simply, we must have faith and also work hard.

We need faith in the power of God. In the book of Mark, chapter 9, verses 22 and 23, Jesus was talking to the father of a boy who had been subject to convulsions since childhood. The man asked Jesus, "But if you can do anything, take pity on us and help us! And Jesus said to him 'If you can!' All things are possible to him who believes."

But you ask, "How do we maintain faith over a seemingly long period of time?" The simple answer is to pray purposefully and sincerely without ceasing, and to keep that faith *forever*. I am reminded of a lady who lived on a farm near ours in my youth. She had lost almost 100 percent of her hearing capacities. She attended the healing revival meeting of an evangelist. Most of her hearing was restored through prayer. The evangelist told her that as long as she kept her faith her hearing would remain good, but if she lost her faith, then her hearing would go with it.

According to the seventeenth chapter of Luke verse 5, the apostles said to the Lord. "Increase our faith!" Then, in the sixth verse, "And the Lord said, 'If you have faith like a mustard seed, you would say to this mulberry tree, Be uprooted and be planted in the sea, and it would obey you.' "

I gain strength when I read James, chapter 1, the second and third verses, "Consider it all joy, my brethren, when you encounter various trials, . . . Knowing that the testing of your faith produces endurance."

Is faith a developed reality? Can we *touch* faith?

I have faith that Timmy will speak words to me someday, and that will be a day of great rejoicing. I had faith that his left arm would move—it is moving now. I also had faith that his left eye would gain vision someday—it has vision now. I told someone recently that, after his hands and arms started to show flexing and usage, we would start to work with his legs and feet—twisted as they are.

Remember I told you in chapter 5 that Timmy's body shook twice while we were praying together holding hands? I had faith that Jesus was working in the life of this youth.

Just last night Timmy and I were talking (in our way) at a Valentine's Day party at the nursing home. This nursing home organization really does so much for the patients. Also, the Heart Association benefited from this party. Timmy turned to me and smiled and winked. Oh, oh, what's coming now, I wondered. I knew that he wanted me to notice something. Immediately I saw a MIRACLE happen: his right foot—the most misshapen of the two—was slowly moving up. Subsequently, his right leg was being lifted off the wheelchair in which he was sitting with both legs outstretched. Then slowly the leg came to rest on the chair, and the foot returned to its original position. Was I seeing things? This act was unbelievable. If you could see his condition you would agree with me.

"Do that again, Timmy, please." I was excited. I wanted to be sure that spasms were not the actual cause of this miracle. The leg and foot rose again, just as before. He smiled and winked. Now I knew that Timmy was doing something different, for the first time.

The chief administrator walked by and stopped to greet Timmy. When I told him of the recent miracle he smiled.

"Timmy, will you please Mr. McArt by raising your right foot and leg again?" I held Timmy's right hand as both of us looked at him expectantly.

"Praise the Lord," was the prayerful response of Mr. McArt, as he saw the right leg rise slowly after the foot had almost straightened out.

Yes, I have faith that miracles will continue to occur with Timmy.

I have read that there were forty-three miracles performed by Jesus in the healing of physical and mental problems as listed in Matthew, Mark, Luke, and John. Also, there were nineteen instances of His command over elements of nature, and seven examples of reviving the dead. Some of these might have been duplicates as seen by the different writers in the Gospels. But certainly there were many more miracles performed by Jesus when these disciples might not have been in His presence. We have read that Jesus went about His work performing miracles and preaching.

Paul, in Ephesians, said that we should take up the shield of faith. We *must* grab and hold on to the shield of faith.

Now, is it possible to have Faith without Love? Do they both go together? Can we have Love without Caring? Something to think about, believe me. Interspersed in among all of these must be the power of Prayer.

We talked about Prayer and Faith. A separate book would not even begin to cover each item. And Love and Care would entail countless volumes. So all we can do in this short story is to emphasize the importance of these things in our lives, and the results that may be realized in using them with Timmy.

You have seen in previous chapters how Love and Care and Prayer and Faith have resulted in unexpected advances or miracles, as I call them. What do you call them?

Is Faith helping Timmy? Do you believe it? Did Faith take over when science slowed down? Or is it time alone that is helping? Does Love and Care mean Timmy's success? Or is it a combination of all of these, including Prayer?

"Let love of the brethren continue. Do not neglect to show hospitality to strangers, for by this some have entertained angels without knowing it." (Hebrews 13:1-2)

What greater love has been exemplified than that in John, chapter 3, verse 16? If you are not sure of this verse, look it up, and read it, and reread it.

I like to think of that passage from 1 John, chapter 4, verse 7,

"Beloved, let us love one another, for love is from God; and every one who loves is born of God and knows God."

Are you a teenager, or over sixty? What does it matter? Are you just sitting around to die or waiting for the right person to come along to love? God calls you to do something in the meantime and all of the time. What might that be? Pray about it. Remember that we are to be used by God in one way or another. Do you believe that?

Can you faithfully say, "Here am I, take me. Help me to have Faith to work for You in Love and Caring."

What about Timmy, our hero?

I am not going to give up in working with him as long as I am able to do so. However, the odds of Timmy's future progress seem to depend a great deal upon Prayer, Faith, Love and Caring.

Aren't you glad that no one pulled the plug when Timmy was critically injured? I am. So I suggest to you who may be responsible someday—wait, don't pull that plug!

Pray for Timmy, *PLEASE*!

Also pray, love, and care for your loved ones. The Rewards may be great sometime. Have Faith.